P9-ECU-175

THE BRONTËS

GREAT LIVES

To be published shortly

Other volumes in preparation

THE BRONTËS
by IRENE COOPER WILLIS

Great Lives

PR
4168
W5

NEW YORK
THE MACMILLAN COMPANY
1933

Made *and* printed *in* Great Britain
By The Camelot Press Ltd
London *and* Southampton

6921

To
N. N.

For a great deal of the information given in this book about the Brontës' juvenile writings, I am most indebted to Miss Fanny Ratchford, Brontë Research Student at the Wrenn Library, University of Texas, Austin, U.S.A. The extent of Miss Ratchford's work on the microscopic manuscripts is outlined by her in an article in the Publications of the Modern Language Association of America, Vol. XLIII (1928), and I have also been much enlightened by a valuable letter from Miss Ratchford on this subject.

I. C. W.

September 1932.

CONTENTS

CHRONOLOGY

Patrick Brontë, born *March* 17*th*, 1777.

Maria Branwell, born 1783.

Patrick Brontë, married to Maria Branwell *December* 29*th*, 1812.

Maria Brontë, born 1813.

Elizabeth Brontë, born 1815.

Charlotte Brontë, born *April* 21*st*, 1816.

Patrick Branwell Brontë, born *June* 26*th*, 1817.

Emily Jane Brontë, born *July* 30*th*, 1818.

Anne Brontë, born *January* 17*th*, 1820.

The family moved from Thornton to Haworth *April* 1820.

Mrs. Brontë, died *September* 15*th*, 1821.

Miss Branwell came to Haworth 1821.

Maria, Elizabeth, Charlotte and Emily at Cowan Bridge School, 1824–5.

Maria Brontë, died *May* 6*th*, 1825.

Elizabeth Brontë, died *June* 15*th*, 1825.

Charlotte at Roe Head School, *January* 1831.

Leaves Roe Head, *July* 1832.

Returns to Roe Head as governess, with Emily, *July* 1835.

Emily leaves Roe Head ; Anne takes her place ; Branwell visits London, 1835–6.

Emily at Halifax as governess for six months, 1836.

Anne Brontë becomes governess at Mrs. Ingham's, *April* 1839.

Charlotte, governess at Mrs. Sidgwick's, 1839.

Charlotte's second situation as governess with Mrs. White, *March* 1841.

Charlotte and Emily go to Brussels, *February* 1842.

Miss Branwell, died *October* 29*th*, 1842.

Charlotte and Emily return to Haworth, *November* 1842.

Charlotte returns to Brussels, *January* 1843.

Returns to Haworth, *January* 1844.

Anne and Branwell at Thorp Green, 1845.

Poems by Currer, Ellis and Acton Bell, published 1846.

Jane Eyre, published *October* 1847.

Wuthering Heights and *Agnes Grey*, published *December* 1847.

Charlotte and Anne visit London, *July* 1848.

Tenant of Wildfell Hall, published 1848.

Branwell, died *September* 24*th*, 1848.

Emily, died *December* 19*th*, 1848.

Anne, died, at Scarborough, *May* 28*th*, 1849.

Shirley, published 1849.

Villette, published 1852.

Charlotte married Mr. Nicholls, *June* 29*th*, 1854.

Charlotte, died *March* 31*st*, 1855.

Rev. Patrick Brontë, died *June* 7*th*, 1861.

CHAPTER I

Here is the ancient floor
Footworn and hollowed and thin,
Here is the former door
Where the dead feet walked in.
                    THOMAS HARDY
                        "The Self Unseeing."

HAWORTH PARSONAGE, where the Brontës lived
and all of them, except Anne, died, has been
open to the public since 1928. Formerly, after
clambering through the steep Yorkshire village
and turning up the lane beside the Church, along-
side the grim churchyard, the visitor could only
peer sideways at the Parsonage which stood above
the churchyard, separated from it by a low wall
and a patch of front grass and shrub. The pilgrim, going to Haworth for the first time, laden
with all that books could tell about the Brontës,
intent with hopes and dreams that Haworth itself
would tell him more, was pulled up short of his
goal. He could not intrude upon the reigning
parson's property and privacy ; he had to make-
shift with a timid view from the lane of an inex-
pressive grey house whose chief feature seemed to
be an array of windows facing the garden and
churchyard below. The house was solidly built.
There was nothing insignificant or mean about its
appearance. It was of a larger, better type than

any other in the village. But still it was a mere, grey, dull-looking house, revealing nothing of its history to the ardent gazer beyond that it was, undoubtedly, the Parsonage, as such it was built, in the eighteenth century, and, for sixty years and more after the Rev. Patrick Brontë's death in 1861, remained.

.   .   .   .

Now the house is a Memorial Museum. The pilgrim opens the gate, walks along the path under the windows of the room which used to be Mr. Brontë's study, and enters. It is a romantic experience, this entrance into a house which in every sense except the actual he already knows. He needs no guide. He hesitates in the hall only from a kind of fear, fear lest his spiritual acquaintance with the house should blot out for him the impression of sight. For it is just this impression he is after. What he has wanted for so long and has come to Haworth to get has been the exact look of the inside of the Parsonage, the exact look of the rooms, their look-out upon that front patch, grey churchyard and tower, the experience of moving about in the house, *being* actually *in* the Brontës' home. There is a touching collection of relics now in the Parsonage, bits of furniture once belonging to the Brontës, dresses of Charlotte's, a trunk, all sorts of family belongings and some of the microscopic manuscripts. But the pilgrim is less occupied with these tangible relics than with the intangible echoes, resonances and reverberations that seem to him to be gathered there. These odds and ends in glass cases, a mug labelled as Emily's, scraps of china, old Brontë's spectacles, who knows how and when they were used, whether they were valued ? But the rooms, their adjacency, the views from them of the village, these are as they always were ; the pilgrim can go about the house, up and down the stone staircase, moving across the same distances, led by the same fundamental impressions as the Brontës had. As he stands on the stairs, the light which slants in from the window behind is the light of *their* afternoons. Lingering on in the house while the shadows on the walls alter, he loses a little the feeling of being a mere visitor and returning to it the next day, he gains more confidence, until it seems as if his relationship with the Parsonage had really become a little bit like what *theirs* must have been.

The hall, or entrance passage, is bigger than one would think, from Mrs. Gaskell's description. It is quite wide and there is a note of structural style about the arch in it and the easy-turning old stone stair. A tall window above the half-landing of the stair lets in all the afternoon sun. The house is in line with the church ; the front windows, four below, five above, look east. There is plenty of light in the house ; the stone-flagged passage with the arch and the staircase are soft with it. There is no need to think of it as a gloomy place. There are, or rather were, eight rooms in the Parsonage. Since the Brontës' day, a wing has been added on the side next to the lane, but this addition does not much alter the original plan. On the right of the front door, as you go in, is Mr. Brontë's study, where he often took his meals alone and where the girls breakfasted with him. On the left, opposite to the study, is the larger room, with two windows, where the family had their other meals and which was used as a general sitting-room. It was here, at night, that the three girls paced up and down, when work was put away for the day and their father and aunt were safely in bed. Mr. Brontë used to retire early, winding up the clock that stood on the half-landing as he went upstairs, and calling out, as he passed the dining-room door, " Now, children, don't be late." It was here, too, that Emily died, on the sofa which has now come back to the Museum, and here that Charlotte, alone and desolate, wrote her moving preface and biographical note to the new edition of her dead sisters' novels. Behind the dining-room, is a small room with a side window, that used to be called the Peat Room ; afterwards, when Charlotte married, it became Mr. Nicholls' study. Behind Mr. Brontë's study was the kitchen, the happiest place in the house for Charlotte, Branwell, Emily and Anne in childhood ; it was there they spent so much time with the faithful Tabby.

Upstairs, Mr. Brontë's bedroom was over the study ; Aunt Branwell's room, over the dining-room. Between the two, over part of the passage, is a small sort of box-room, which the children used as a nursery or study, and later Emily is said to have slept there. Anne slept with her aunt and Branwell with his father ; Charlotte's bedroom, until Miss Branwell died, must have been over the Peat Room, or over the kitchen, for one of the two back rooms was the servants' bedroom, and in early and later days there were two servants. The back rooms are small, and the box-room, or nursery, is tiny, but the front rooms are fair-sized and the Brontës could not have been overcrowded, except in the first years of their life at the Parsonage when Mrs. Brontë was dying, and the children, six of them then, may have had to be squeezed somehow with the servants into the two back bedrooms.

Haworth itself has been often called " over-described." It is a typical Yorkshire moorland village, bleak and grim to Southern eyes, isolated on a hill-top and foreign. Its people are working-class ; the stone of its buildings, some of it buff-coloured to start with, like that of the new Parsonage on the moor road to Colne, soon becomes dingy ; its ash-trees and firs are stunted and twisted with the moor winds ; its flowers, except for the heather, are few. Though Keighley, four miles away, in the valley, has spread hugely since the Brontës' time, and now the road from there up to Haworth is almost lined with houses, the hill-top still seems solitary because of the great sea of undulating moorland stretching above and beyond. Dun-grey moors under a grey sky rise and fall endlessly to the horizon ; in the foreground, patches of green hillside, ribbed with fences of grey-black stone and dotted here and there with low grey-black stone houses, tell of days when these Yorkshire dales belonged to a few scattered farmers who spun and wove the wool of the sheep of their moors. Below, in the valleys, sprawl smoky manufacturing towns and villages pouring their villainous smoke upwards. Seen from a distance, industrial England has its moments of beauty; some lights can glorify those ugly masses of smoke and smut; the sun from above, or some furnace glare from within, can transfigure the dull coppery and leaden blankets of fog and smoke enwrapping the towns, turn their lividness into ethereal gold haloes against which factories and chimneys stand out dim and spectral shapes.   And the closeness of these big, squalid, sprawling towns to the endless, thunder-cloud-coloured, undulating sea of moorland has a strange charm for the imagination.

CHAPTER II

Mrs. Gaskell, in her *Life of Charlotte Brontë*, written soon after Charlotte's death in 1855, put a vivid touch into her account of the Brontës' arrival in Haworth (in 1820) when she said that there were still people alive in the village who remembered " seven heavily-laden carts lumbering slowly up the long stone street bearing the ' new parson's ' household goods to his future abode."

That caravan, containing, no doubt, the new parson's family as well as his furniture, had come by way of the moors south of Haworth, from Thornton, near Bradford, six miles or so away. For the last five years, Mr. Brontë had been curate of Thornton ; before that, he had been at Hartshead, near Huddersfield, and it was while he was at Hartshead that he had married.

The Reverend Patrick Brontë was an Irishman, born, in 1777, in a cottage at Lisnacreevy, Drumballrooney, County Down. His father, Hugh Brunty, was a peasant-farmer, and Patrick was one of ten brothers and sisters. The family's name and origin have been investigated by several writers, and it seems probable that the ancestral name was O'Prunty. But Hugh's children were entered in the local register when they were baptised under the name of Brunty or Brunte.

Patrick was evidently a bright lad for, at the age of sixteen, after starting work as a weaver, he took to school teaching in a Presbyterian school near his home. From there, he became a teacher in a bigger school at Drumballrooney where the rector encouraged and helped him to aim at Cambridge University and the Church. The young man persevered, and put money by and entered St. John's College, Cambridge, when he was twenty-five. There he took exhibitions and a degree, in 1806, signing the register Patr. Bronte (his name upon entrance is set down as Branty in the college books), and was ordained to a curacy at Wethersfield in Essex. At this stage, he apparently started putting an accent on the last syllable of his surname, perhaps in order to show how it should be pronounced. Later, he changed the accent for two dots, possibly to borrow a little lustre from Lord Nelson's title of Duke of Bronte. This is surmise, but on the other hand, Mr. Brontë had the usual human weakness for " birth." He was fond of saying that he had been at Cambridge and at the same college with Lord Palmerston, and, from some details which have been published of an early love affair between him and a young woman, Mary Burder, at Wethersfield, it appears that he was secretive about his Irish relations and given to bragging to her of his affluent and titled friends. The secretiveness was partly responsible for the break-up of the love affair. Mary Burder, it seems, had a worldly uncle who had no intention of allowing his niece, who was well provided for, to marry an Irish curate who kicked at questions about his parentage, and by his ruthless machinations the lovers were parted, never to meet again. Mr. Brontë may have found Wethersfield unbearable after this disappointment for, in 1809, he departed to a curacy at Wellington. He did not, however, stay long at Wellington ; he soon went on to Yorkshire where, before being appointed to Harts-head, he was for more than a year curate to the Rev. John Buckworth, Vicar of Dewsbury.

Except for the Mary Burder episode which came to grief through no lack of ardour on the part of either of the lovers, little is known about Mr. Brontë in these years until he met and married the mother of his famous family, in 1812. A few stories have been raked from the memories of acquaintances and parishioners : he knocked a bully down, on one occasion ; he rescued a child who fell into a river ; he took a leading part in petitioning for the release of a young man who had been wrongly convicted. He attended to his clerical duties and was respected. In 1811, he published a small book of *Cottage Poems*, and during the next seven years, another book of poems and two books of prose tales, all very dull and didactic, came from his pen. Still, as Mr. Shorter says, he seems to have given himself no airs in consequence of being an author, and as it was, no doubt, their father's example and taste for writing which made the young Brontës start writing so early, these dull tales and duller verses have, at any rate, historical interest.

Maria Branwell, who married the Irish curate of Hartshead, was a Cornish woman. She was visiting an uncle and aunt, Mr. and Mrs. John Fennell, who presided over a Wesleyan academy near Bradford, when she met Mr. Brontë. Her parents, respectable Penzance citizens, and Methodists, were dead ; she was twenty-nine years of age, her own mistress, with a small annuity. Her young cousin, Jane Fennell, was already engaged to another curate, Mr. Morgan, who was a friend of Patrick Brontë's, and this circumstance no doubt helped to bring about Maria's engagement. The two weddings took place together at Guiseley Church on December 29th, 1812, and each bridegroom officiated to marry the other.

Many years afterwards, Mr. Brontë gave Charlotte a packet of her mother's letters written to him during the courtship, and they are published in Mr. Clement Shorter's book. They are the letters of a young woman carefully trained in the long-winded pieties and proprieties of Methodist circles of that time, but with a quiet individuality and evidently warmly attached to her future husband whom, on one occasion, she is daring enough to call her " dear, saucy Pat." Unfortunately the corresponding letters from Mr. Brontë to Maria Branwell were not preserved – the bereaved husband may have burnt them after her death – for it would have been interesting to examine them for evidence of sauciness and other unclerical qualities which are hinted at by some of Maria's gentle remarks. Though it is now recognised that there is nothing substantial behind the charge of violent eccentricity that Mrs. Gaskell at first brought against Mr. Brontë, and that other writers from time to time have chosen to maintain, one need only look at Mr. Brontë's photographs – there are several taken in old age besides one of him as a younger man – to see that he had a marked individuality such as might easily have issued in unclerical behaviour. He was, however, a man of considerable outward dignity and character. He had a regard for education, of the kind that had raised him from an Irish cabin to the Church, but, to judge from his literary productions, he was without any originality or distinction of mind, and his eccentricities, on which so much stress has been laid, do not seem much more than relics of the crude goings on of the peasant class from which he came. His writings are so commonplace that it is odd to hear that their author used to regale the breakfast table with lurid tales, the more startling, perhaps, for a visitor, by being told by a silver-haired clergyman, erect in broadcloth and huge choker cravat, within sight, through the breakfast-room windows, of his own church and grim churchyard. Many of these tales, according to Dr. William Wright, author of *The Brontës in Ireland*, were from the rich store of Grandfather Brunty, the peasant Hugh in Ireland, who, from the same account, was a remarkable character as well as a famous storyteller. Mr. Brontë, whether or not he inherited his father's imagination, had, anyway, harvested from boyhood's days a collection of fearful tales and legends which, when in social mood, he would retail, to Emily's especial relish, Miss Nussey remembered. Emily was supposed to be like her father. That fierce determination of hers is more likely, certainly, to have come from him than from the mother. Mr. Brontë's violence was screened by a dignified manner which a sense of the position which he had reached had imposed on his early ambition and impetuous blood. He had no mental flexibility; no sympathetic imagination; his thought was purely platitudinous, characteristics which a certain independence of judgment in practical, parochial matters and his so-called eccentricities of conduct could easily, on slight acquaintance, hide. As suggested, his eccentricities, such as keeping a loaded pistol by him and discharging it daily, snipping out the sleeves of one of his wife's dresses because he disliked the shape, and his horror of fire, to the extent of forbidding curtains to the windows, were only odd, judged by genteel standards; they may have been quite common traits in County Down. His was a patchy gentility, acquired under difficulties and never enlarged into the full-dress respectabilities of his professional brethren. Peasant habits, strong as the brogue of his speech, often came uppermost above the choker and broadcloth.

The newly married couple took up their abode at Hartshead, where the two eldest children, Maria and Elizabeth, were born. In 1815, Mr. Brontë exchanged livings with the curate of

Thornton, and at Thornton were born Charlotte, on April 21st, 1816 ; Patrick Branwell, on June 26th, 1817 ; Emily Jane, on July 30th, 1818, and Anne, on January 17th, 1820. There were, therefore, six children under the age of seven, the youngest a baby about three months old, stowed away in one of those carts that lumbered up the village street of Haworth in April of 1820 and, taking the turning by the church, unloaded at the door of the Parsonage.

Curious, and perhaps some hostile or, at all events, critical eyes watched that procession and arrival. There had been a rumpus in the parish over the presentation of Mr. Brontë to the living. This was not on grounds of personal objection to him but because the presentation and the control of funds which provided part of the parson's stipend were in different hands, and the local Trustees of the latter had not, apparently, been consulted as to the appointment. Mr. Brontë, to avoid difficulties on this account, kept himself strictly within his duties when he first went to Haworth. He commenced these, two months or so before he removed his wife and family from Thornton ; he may have waited, on account of these troubles, to shift the household, or because, in February, his wife had not yet recovered from the birth of the last baby.

Circumstances, therefore, at the outset, were against any very friendly relationship being established between the Parsonage and the village, and Mrs. Brontë's illness from cancer which started not long afterwards must have kept the situation, as regards social intercourse, much as it was at the start.

Mrs. Brontë fell ill in January 1821 ; she died in September 1821, after " seven months of agonising illness." This we know from a letter, recently discovered to have been written by Mr. Brontë, which was published in the *Cottage Magazine* of 1822. The letter was entitled : " A Letter from a Clergyman – In answer to a letter of sympathy on the loss of his wife." Only the initial letters of names were originally printed, but Mr. C. W. Hatfield, the authority on Brontë MSS., has no doubt of its authorship and it was reprinted in the *Transactions of the Brontë Society*, 1931. From this letter, several hitherto unknown facts emerge as to Mrs. Brontë's illness and death, and life, during that sad time, at the Parsonage. It was not previously known that Miss Elizabeth Branwell came from Penzance to look after her sister's family some months before the death of Mrs. Brontë. Mrs. Gaskell stated, as she had been told, that Miss Branwell arrived to take charge of the household a year or so after her sister's death, and all writers on the Brontës have naturally repeated what Mrs. Gaskell said. Miss Branwell may not, of course, have arrived to take up her permanent abode at Haworth until later, but we now know that she came earlier to look after the family, while her sister was dying.

" For the first three months " (of his wife's illness), Mr. Brontë writes, " I was left nearly quite alone, unless you suppose my six little children, and the nurse and servants, to have been company. Had I been at D(ewsbury) I should not have wanted kind friends ; had I been at H(artshead) I should have seen them, and others, occasionally ; or had I been at T(hornton), a family there, who were ever truly kind, would have soothed my sorrows ;   but I   was   at H(aworth), a stranger in a strange land.   It was under these circumstances, after every earthly prop was removed, that I was called on to bear the weight of the greatest load of sorrows that ever pressed upon me.   One day, I remember it well, it was a gloomy day, a day of clouds and darkness, three of my little children were taken ill of scarlet fever; and the day after, the remaining three were in the same condition.   Just at that time, death seemed to have laid his hand on my dear wife in a manner which threatened her speedy dissolution.   She was cold and silent, and seemed hardly to notice what was passing around her. This awful season, however, was not of long duration.   My little children had a favourable turn, and at length got well ; and the force of my wife's disease somewhat abated.   A few weeks afterwards, her sister Miss B(ranwell) arrived, and afforded great comfort to my mind, which has been the case ever since, by sharing my labours and sorrows, and behaving as an affectionate mother to my children."   (The letter is dated November 27th, 1821, more than two months after Mrs. Brontë's death, and evidently Miss Branwell was still there.)   Mr. Brontë went on to say that he called in different doctors but they could do nothing for the sufferer. "After above seven months of more agonising pain than I ever saw anyone endure," she died. He evidently felt his wife's death terribly : "There were seasons," he says, "when an affectionate, agonising something, sickened my whole frame" and "could not be described." "And when my dear wife was dead and buried and gone, and when I missed her at every corner, and when her memory was hourly revived by the innocent, yet distressing prattle of my children . . . I was happy at the recollection that to sorrow, not as those without hope, was no sin." He then tells his correspondent, the Vicar of Dewsbury, of the practical kindness of friends who sent him money to meet the expenses and debts incurred during the illness. He had received in all £250. This shows that Mr. Brontë had good friends and also that his wife had, as he said, the best medical attention and nursing that he could provide for her, both of which facts go counter to the legend of him as a violent eccentric who bullied his wife and insisted on such meagre fare for the children that they suffered all their lives from under-nourishment in infancy. There is no basis for the legend. Mr. Brontë "was perhaps peculiar " – as one of his wife's Cornish nieces wrote to Mr. Shorter – but, she added, she had always heard her mother (a sister of Mrs. Brontë's) say that he was devotedly fond of his wife and she of him. The stories were mischievous village gossip, at most, gross exaggerations and distortions of facts. Mr. Brontë *did* regularly keep a pistol by him and discharge it, but as he had been a curate in districts where there had been Luddite disturbances this was not surprising, added to which he seems always to have taken a schoolboyish delight in fire-arms. He did, on one occasion, snip out the sleeves of one of his wife's dresses because they were not to his taste, but he forthwith purchased silk for a new dress in the place of the one he had spoiled and Mrs. Brontë apparently took the matter as a joke. He may not have been a lovable father : he was not warm-hearted (nor were any of his children) but, according to his lights and temperament, he was not unkind. He held narrow views, he thought dancing and card-playing were sinful—but so did so many people in those days, and no doubt the atmosphere of the Parsonage was much more repressive and didactic than sympathetic and stimulating to those six small children whose " innocent prattle " Mr. Brontë found so distressing after his wife's death. He was no child lover ; his pride and aim were to make the children into little grown-ups as soon as possible and he succeeded. Long before Maria, the eldest, died at the age of eleven, her father, according to Mrs. Gaskell, " could converse with her on any of the leading topics of the day with as much freedom and pleasure as with any grown-up person " and, in the often quoted account of how it occurred to Mr. Brontë to test the children's knowledge by making each of them in turn answer questions under cover of a mask (which, he thought, would conquer their shyness), Anne, a mite of four, was as quick as her sisters and brother to see that an impressive utterance was expected of her and replied, oracularly, when asked what a child like her most wanted : " Age and experience." All the answers which were of this kind made a deep impression on Mr. Brontë, so he told Mrs. Gaskell. He had, he said, often thought before that the children were unusually talented but until then he had evidently not realised what perfect little echoes of elderly platitudes his six little pitchers had become.

It must have been soon after the mask experiment that the two elder girls, Maria and Elizabeth, then aged ten and nine, were taken by their father to the Cowan Bridge School where, a few weeks later, Charlotte, aged eight, and Emily, six, were also conducted. The Clergy Daughters School, to give it its proper name, was partly a charity school – the small fees being supplemented by charitable subscriptions – and its presiding authority, Mr. Carus Wilson, an Evangelical clergyman, quite evidently held views concerning the education of the young which deserved the portrait of him, in Charlotte's *Jane Eyre*, as " the black, marble clergyman." The children were probably no worse looked after and fed than they would have been in any other similar institution in those days. Piety of the dreariest kind and indifference to physical comforts were the rule in such places. Lamb and Coleridge had fared no better at the Bluecoat School twenty years or so earlier. Maria and Elizabeth arrived at Cowan Bridge, apparently, scarcely recovered from measles and whooping-cough and whether, in

consequence of insufficient and badly cooked food
and Spartan treatment, or because they were
delicate to start with, or perhaps because of both
these reasons, they were taken ill at the school
and died soon after they were fetched home.
Maria left in February 1825, and died in May ;
Elizabeth was brought home at the end of May
and died a fortnight later. Charlotte and Emily
were taken away by Mr. Brontë the day after
Elizabeth was removed ; they were both back at
Haworth when Elizabeth died. Charlotte never
forgot her impressions of that time and drew upon
them for the picture of Lowood in *Jane Eyre*, and
in that story, the saintly Helen Burns was Maria,
as nearly as Charlotte could remember her much
loved sister. With such a sister, acting the little
mother to them all since their real mother's death,
the children's early years could not have been
unhappy, though to us they seem pathetic. Charlotte barely remembered her mother ; she had
only an isolated memory of her playing once in
the evening light with Branwell in the parlour.
Branwell was between Charlotte and Emily.
Emily was just three when her mother died –
Anne a year and a half old – so that probably
none of the recollections of these four younger
children even brushed on that monotonous hushed
time we are so often told of when the six children
were bundled into the tiny nursery, next door to
where the mother lay dying, and told to play
quietly. Distinct memories may not have begun
for any of them, except Maria and Elizabeth,
until Aunt Branwell was well established at the

Parsonage, with her work, no doubt, cut out to
substitute her prim authority for the gentle rule
of good, untidy Maria. Clearer against these dim
beginnings for Charlotte and Emily must have
been the Lowood tragedy, the epidemic of sickness at the school, the disappearance of Maria and
Elizabeth, the sudden, solemn return home, the
dramatic first meeting with death.

After Cowan Bridge, for the next six years, until
Charlotte went to school again in 1831, Aunt
Branwell's rule settled over the schoolroom, or
rather over the lessons conducted in the bedroom
(formerly Mrs. Brontë's bedroom) where she spent
so much of the day. The downstairs rooms and
staircase were stone-flagged ; a sore grievance
with " Aunt," who stayed much upstairs in consequence and clicked about on pattens whenever
she had to descend. Her rule was prim and fussy
but not destructive of personality, or otherwise
the children could not have been so devoted to
their home. She made pets of the boy, Branwell,
and Anne, the baby. Charlotte and Emily,
though they respected, never really cared for
" Aunt."

Mr. Brontë made two attempts to marry again.
He applied first to his old love, Mary Burder of
Wethersfield, but she refused his offer. From a
correspondence between them (published in the
Sphere, August 30th, 1913), apparently something
in the past rankled in her mind. She twitted him
about " those great and affluent friends you used
to write and speak of " and then she said, mysteri-
ously : " Your confidence I have never betrayed,

strange as was the disclosure you once made to me." Our curiosity as to the "strange disclosure" must remain unsatisfied, for Mr. Brontë merely replied, several months afterwards: "I confessed to you that I had done some things which I was sorry for which originated chiefly in very difficult circumstances which surrounded me and which were produced chiefly by myself." Miss Burder became Mrs. Peter Sibree of Wethersfield and the correspondence was not renewed.

It is said that Miss Elizabeth Firth of Thornton was also sought by Mr. Brontë in marriage, without success. She was not more than twenty-five when Mrs. Brontë died, and as a girl of eighteen onwards had taken the liveliest interest in the Brontë family when they lived at Thornton where the Firths also lived. A diary which she kept from 1816–1820 was published by her grandson, Professor Moore Smith of Sheffield, in the *Bookman* for October 1904, and it reveals how very often the Firths and Brontës called on one another and "took tea." It reveals too that Miss Branwell stayed with her sister and brother-in-law for over a year at Thornton, and partook of the tea drinking and other social pleasures there, which explains why Miss Branwell afterwards found Haworth (where there were no tea-parties) extremely dull. The Firths were generous friends to the Brontës and though Miss Firth's schoolgirl interest in her former pastor and his family did not go so far as to enable her to become the second Mrs. Brontë ("her heart," says Professor

Moore Smith, " was engaged elsewhere "), she always took the kindest interest in the children, the godmother of some of whom she had been, and had them to stay with her at Huddersfield when she married the vicar of that town. On her wedding tour, in 1824, she called at the Cowan Bridge School and gave, as she entered in her account book, " 3 Miss Brontës, 2s. 6d. each." She died in 1837.

Mr. Brontë resigned himself to widowerhood and became elderly and dyspeptic. He was not a genial man at the best of times, though when fortune smiled he could make a show of sociability as in the Thornton days. But the misfortune which had cut short his married life and stranded him with a family of young children, whom he had no idea how to love or to educate except by conversing with them on the leading topics of the day, was too much for him. He retired to his study, and though he did his duty by his parishioners and was liked by them the better for doing no more than his duty, he cultivated a poor digestion and invalidish habits, frequently taking his meals alone. He took charge of Branwell's lessons – as a young man he had been a schoolmaster – but in the bosom of his family, when he was not being sententious or bad tempered, he was silent and grim.

Miss Branwell, out of a sense of duty to her sister's children, remained on at the Parsonage. She was not afraid of her brother-in-law and as she had a small annuity of £50 a year, the position, in some respects, may have been to her liking, though she was much given to harping on the far-away charms of her native Penzance. It may have been out of such harpings that Emily's fierce love for Haworth grew, and out of that, later, the Gondal saga, for the Gondals inhabited northern regions in contradistinction to Charlotte's and Branwell's Angrians who ruled in the sunny south.

The children's home life centred much more round Tabby's kitchen than Papa's study or Aunt's bedroom. Tabby (Tabitha Ackroyd) came to be servant at the Parsonage about 1825. She was then fifty-four, a Yorkshire woman of the old type, born and bred in Haworth, remembering the days when packhorses jingled through the village and fairies were to be seen, on moonlight nights, dancing by the stream in the valley bottom where the mills now were. The children were her " bairns " ; she ruled them pretty sharply, says Mrs. Gaskell, but she never grudged trouble to give them treats. The kitchen was evidently where, as often as not, they collected ; and, as one of Charlotte's first chronicles shows, it was round the kitchen fire that their fancies sprouted and at the kitchen table that Charlotte, at any rate, started to write.

CHAPTER III

THERE were not too many books in the Parsonage and Charlotte was probably drawing from memory in *Shirley* when she described the " collection of light literature " which Caroline Helstone had access to at Briarfield Rectory as " chiefly contained on a shelf which had belonged to her Aunt Mary : some venerable *Lady's Magazines* that had once performed a sea-voyage with their owner and whose pages were stained with salt water : some mad Methodist magazines, full of miracles and apparitions, of preternatural warnings, ominous dreams and frenzied fanaticism : the equally mad Letters of Mrs. Elizabeth Rowe from the Dead to the Living : a few old English classics." Mrs. Brontë, of Methodist upbringing, might well have had such a collection and the reference to salt water damage tallies with the mention in one of her love-letters that a box of her belongings had been shipwrecked on its journey by sea from Cornwall to Yorkshire.

Keighley, however, had a lending library which the family, as they grew up, made use of, and Mrs. Gaskell tells how the girls used to tramp to the town and back again to get a new book

6921

which they would dip into on their way home. But, in childhood, this could not have happened often – the walk to Keighley and back was eight miles – and the children, like Caroline Helstone, had to make do with the oddments of literature at home which seem, anyway, to have included Sir Walter Scott's works, Wordsworth's and Southey's poems, *Pilgrim's Progress*, the *Arabian Nights*, and *Æsop's Fables*. A copy of Scott's *Tales of a Grandfather* in three volumes exists with an inscription in Miss Branwell's handwriting : "A New Year's Gift by Miss E. B. to her dear little nephew and nieces, Patrick, Charlotte, Emily and Anne Brontë, 1828." Miss Branwell saw to it that no time should be spent in reading until the allotted tasks of house-work and sewing were duly performed, but Mr. Brontë approved of reading and ever since the children could remember they had shared his keen interest in politics. He was, of course, a strong Tory and his views on Reform, as to which all England was then agitated, can be imagined, as also on Catholic Emancipation, until the great Duke saw fit to concede a measure to this end himself. Charlotte, aged thirteen or so, has drawn a vivid picture of Parsonage excitement during this period in one of her early writings : " I remember the day when the Intelligence Extraordinary came with Mr. Peel's speech in it, containing the terms on which the Catholics were to be let in. With what eagerness papa tore off the cover, and how we all gathered round him, and with what breathless anxiety we listened, as one by one they were disclosed and explained and argued upon so ably and so well, and then when it was all out, how aunt said that she thought it was excellent and that the Catholics could do no harm with such good security. I remember also the doubts as to whether it would pass the House of Lords and the prophecies that it would not, and when the paper came which was to decide the question, the anxiety was almost dreadful with which we listened to the whole affair ; the opening of the doors ; the hush ; the royal dukes in their robes and the great Duke in green sash and waistcoat ; the rising of all the peeresses when he rose ; the reading of his speech – papa saying that his words were like precious gold ; and lastly the majority . . . in favour of the Bill."

The newspapers were devoured, also *Blackwood's Magazine*, but recently started and flashing with Ambrosian wit and satire. From Blackwood's pages came, we may be sure, many an inspiration, of plot or phrase, for the development of the Verdopolitan and Angrian literature which Charlotte from 1829 onwards was furiously producing. In earlier days, the children were given to acting plays of their own invention, wherein, according to Mr. Brontë, Charlotte's hero, the Duke of Wellington, used always to come off conqueror ; the others' heroes being Buonaparte, Hannibal and Cæsar. One of Charlotte's first chronicles, *The History of the Year*, is quoted by Mrs. Gaskell and starts, as children's writings so often do when the desire to write, no matter what, is strong, with an exact setting down of what is going on round them at the moment. (This childish habit persists in Emily's and Anne's later chronicles.) "While I write this," Charlotte writes (March 12th, 1829), "I am in the kitchen of the Parsonage, Haworth. Tabby, the servant, is washing up the breakfast things, and Anne, my youngest sister (Maria was my eldest), is kneeling on a chair, looking at some cakes which Tabby has been baking for us. Emily is in the parlour, brushing the carpet. Papa and Branwell are gone to Keighley. Aunt is upstairs in her room and I am sitting by the table writing in the kitchen." Having dealt with immediate surroundings, Charlotte perhaps bit her pen and looked further afield. " Keighley," she goes on, " is a small town four miles from here. Papa and Branwell are gone for the newspaper, the *Leeds Intelligencer*, a most excellent Tory newspaper, edited by Mr. Wood and the proprietor, Mr. Henneman. We take two and see three newspapers a week. We take the *Leeds Intelligencer*, Tory, and the *Leeds Mercury*, Whig, edited by Mr. Baines and his brother, son-in-law and two sons, Edward and Talbot. We see the *John Bull* ; it is a high Tory, very violent. Mr. Driver lends us it, as likewise *Blackwood's Magazine*, the most able periodical there is. The editor is Mr. Christopher North, an old man, seventy-four years of age : the 1st of April is his birthday : his company are Timothy Tickler, Morgan O'Doherty, Macrabin Mordecai, Mullion, Warnell and James Hogg, a man of most extraordinary genius, a Scottish shepherd." She then plunges into more important

matters : " Our plays were established : *Young
Men*, June 1826 ; *Our Fellows*, July 1827 ; *Islanders*,
December 1827. These are our three great plays
that are not kept secret. Emily's and my bed
plays were established, Dec. 1, 1827 ; the others
March 1828. Bed plays mean secret plays ;
they are very nice ones. All our plays are very
strange ones. Their nature I need not write on
paper for I think I shall always remember them.
The *Young Men's* play took its rise from some
wooden soldiers Branwell had ; *Our Fellows* from
Æsop's Fables ; and the *Islanders* from several
events which happened. I will sketch out the
origin of our plays more explicitly if I can.
First *Young Men*. Papa bought Branwell some
wooden soldiers at Leeds : when papa came home
it was night, and we were in bed, so next morning
Branwell came to our door with a box of soldiers.
Emily and I jumped out of bed, and I snatched
up one and exclaimed ' This is the Duke of
Wellington. This shall be the Duke.' When I
had said this Emily likewise took up one and said
it should be hers ; when Anne came down she
said one should be hers. Mine was the prettiest
of the whole, and the tallest and the most perfect
in every part. Emily's was a grave looking fellow,
and we called him ' Gravey.' Anne's was a
queer little thing, much like herself, and we called
him ' Waiting-boy.' Branwell chose his and called
him Buonaparte."

It was out of this play centring round the toy
soldiers that the so-called Angrian literature developed, though Angria, that imaginary kingdom

in Africa, did not emerge at the very beginning. Twelveston, later called Glasstown, Verreopolis or Verdopolis, was the first invention. This was the gorgeous city on the banks of the River Niger which the Twelve Heroes, represented by the toy soldiers, built with the help of their Guardian Genii, Talli (Charlotte), Branni (Branwell), Emmi (Emily) and Anni (Anne), after being shipwrecked on the African coast and after battling with the black inhabitants of those regions. Glasstown grew by magic ; it soon became the most marvellous city in the world, beautiful beyond compare, palatial in its buildings, imperial in its control and influence, the magnificent Capital of a Confederacy of Kingdoms ruled by the original Twelve or their descendants, under the leadership of the Duke of Wellington. The Duke, however, did not long remain the central figure ; he was eclipsed by his eldest son, Lord Arthur Augustus Adrian Wellesley, Marquis of Douro, Duke of Zamorna, King of Angria, Emperor Adrian, a wildly Byronic hero whose achievements in military, political, social and domestic spheres were followed and recorded with a mixture of violent admiration and equally violent jealousy and scorn by his younger brother, Lord Charles Albert Florian Wellesley, an inquisitive, suspicious and observant youth, or rather child of about ten years old, with whom Charlotte completely identified herself. Branwell, on the other hand, in the persons of Captain, afterwards Lord, John Flower, Viscount Richton and of Alexander Percy, Earl of Northangerland, was responsible for the political and revolutionary changes which from time to time played havoc with Zamorna's fate. Douro was originally married to Marian Hume, a simple, lovely maiden of humble birth. The marriage had taken place despite the mad jealousy of Lady Zenobia Ellrington, " the prima donna of the Angrian court, the most learned woman of her age, the modern Cleopatra, the Verdopolitan de Staël," whose great mind had been temporarily unhinged by her passion for the Marquis. Defeated in her schemes for frustrating the marriage, Lady Zenobia marries Percy, Earl of Northangerland and dangles her nobly-born stepdaughter, Mary Percy, before the roving eyes of Douro, who abandons Marian, who dies, broken-hearted. Douro with Percy's unscrupulous aid has demanded and received three of the richest provinces in the Confederacy in full sovereignty, and as he assumes the ducal, royal and imperial titles in quick succession, he takes on changes in character which make him in the end a compound of oriental despot, Napoleon and Byron. Percy, now Prime Minister of the new nation, is, however, too ambitious to be loyal. He instigates opposition to and criticism of Zamorna : the Press and Parliament rock with dissensions and crises. To bring Percy to heel, Zamorna threatens to banish his wife, the only person in the world whom her father, Percy, loves. Percy launches civil war and foreign invasion ; Adrianopolis is desolated, the country ravaged ; the Duchess's heart is broken and Zamorna passes into Napoleonic captivity. Such, very briefly, is the outline of the Angrian cycle, or series of stories, dramas, poems and essays which poured from Charlotte between 1829 (when it seems that the demon for scribbling first seized her) and 1840, and to which Branwell contributed, but not, so far as has been discovered, either Emily or Anne. Already, by the end of August 1830, twenty-two volumes had been written (these are the list reproduced by Mrs. Gaskell, drawn up by Charlotte with pedantic precision and entitled " A Catalogue of my books with the period of their completion up to August 30th, 1830,") as well as a long volume by Branwell called *The History of the Young Men*, and six or more numbers of *Branwell's Blackwood Magazine*, written, some by Charlotte, some by Branwell. Most of these books are tiny in size, so made to be in scale with the toy soldiers, their supposed authors, not as has so often been said because the Brontë children were short of paper. The magazines, for instance, are not more than one and a half inches by one and a quarter inches, in size ; other books are three and half inches by four inches, while some are octavo volumes. The texts are written in a minute hand-printing, impossible to read without a magnifying-glass. There are elaborate title pages, prefaces and colophons containing signature and date. The leaves are usually sewed together inside a cover of blue or brown wrapping-paper. Some of the stories have been published in recent years, the latest publication being of *The Spell*, a novel purporting to have been written by Lord Charles Albert Florian Wellesley in 1834, when Charlotte was eighteen. *The Spell* is said by its editor to be " by all means the best " of three pieces contained in a booklet now in the British Museum which was picked up at a sale in Brussels and is supposed, on that account, to have been taken there by Charlotte and given by her to M. Héger. But the trouble with all these early writings is that evidently it is only as a whole (and an amazingly voluminous whole) that they are interesting and even so, only interesting as showing Charlotte's complete absorption in this imaginary world, not as awakening in the reader any interest in, or sympathetic attention to the subject matter. *The Spell*, for instance, is pure bombast ; there is no trace of genuine expression in it ; it might have been written by a child of twelve with a passion for mouthy grandiloquence derived from reading the old-fashioned kind of cheap romantic literature. The mixture of grandiloquence and slang in the dialogue is not even funny, as in the *Irene Iddesleigh* type of novel ; nor is there any of the *naïveté* of *The Young Visiters*. The earlier published writings – *The Twelve Adventurers*, etc., Hodder & Stoughton, 1925 – have not the glaring defects of *The Spell*, but most of them are, nevertheless, pretentious efforts, conscientious meditations upon appropriate themes pursued by Charlotte with touching literary ambition, her young head excitedly full of flowers of rhetoric, borrowed thoughts, borrowed emotions, borrowed impressions, no one of which she had ever realised or examined critically. Charlotte, later, learned to *write*, that is to say to make her readers feel what she was feeling ; but it was Life which taught her that, not books, nor her ten years and more of day-dreaming in Angria. Precocious, in a narrow literary and intellectual sense, she certainly was, but at the same time, as a thinking, feeling human being she was surprisingly backward. Yet not perhaps surprisingly, when it is considered how little contact she, or her brother and sisters, had with any world outside their home. " In the little moorland village where we reside," as Charlotte described Haworth in one of her early letters, there was no social life for the children. They had no playmates except one another ; Branwell mixed with village boys – that could not be prevented – but it would not have been proper for the Parsonage young ladies to play with villagers. Neither Mr. Brontë's nor Miss Branwell's outlook could have been enlivening nor could the occasional visits to Uncle Fennell and Mrs. Franks or parish functions have been much of a corrective to life's everyday poverty. Indeed, Charlotte's immense literary output in childhood and girlhood, as much in volume as all her published novels, is the most pathetic monument to the dull monotony of her actual life in these periods and to the lack of opportunities for natural human development which she and her brother and sisters had at Haworth. The grasp and management of political and social doings which the Angrian literature shows, the historical development of policy and ambitions, the attention paid throughout to exact details of intricate family relationship, in short all the evidence contained

in these books of the young author's intense
absorption in her Angrian heroes and heroines, do
but accentuate the pathetic biographical aspect
of this monument, just as the very perfection of an
elaborate toy carved by a prisoner, or a fine
diamond-scratching of verses on a prison window-
pane make the heart of a sympathetic observer
ache because of the long years spent in captivity
to which such skill testifies. That Charlotte was
fascinated by her game, that it became her one
absorbing pastime, that for years she lived in
that Angrian world, revelling in the Ionic
features, hyacinthine locks and marble brows of
her Douros and Percys, recording their dazzling
careers, flawed by crime and stained with
treachery, wedding them to her Marinas and
Marians and pursuing them with the unbridled
passions of her Lady Zenobias, and succouring
them by the pure devotions of her Mina Laurys ;
that these marvellous, unreal, flaunting, ranting
beings became the consolers of her secret loneliness, whom she could love, clasp, scorn and fight
her fill with, creatures to whom she could give
herself utterly, as we give only to those we have
chosen or created, are of course compensating
facts, but they do not prove that life at Haworth
Parsonage for the young Brontës was not dreary.

Very little is known of Emily's and Anne's play
about the Gondals, owing to the destruction,
either by them, or by Charlotte after their deaths,
of their papers, but the few fragments that have
been found indicate that the Gondal literature
was extensive and it is not therefore straining at

an analogy to suggest that the *Gondal Chronicles*, which so absorbed them in later years, grew out of a play which, following the example of Charlotte and Branwell, they had invented in childhood. Many children are similarly inventive, though it is rare to find childish creations persisting through adolescence and continuing well into the twenties, as happened with the Brontës. The explanation must be sought in their exceptionally isolated circumstances and in their shyness, the result, probably, of isolation. All the Brontës, except Branwell, were morbidly shy, but then Branwell was the only one who had anything like regular contact with the outside world. Charlotte was not shy at home or with friends ; Emily's shyness was more fierce reserve than timidity. It is worth noting that a mention of Emily, aged six, when she was at Cowan Bridge School, by the " Miss Temple " of *Jane Eyre*, makes no reference to her shyness. " Miss Temple " wrote her recollections of the Brontë children to Mrs. Gaskell, and after dwelling on Elizabeth's " exemplary patience " on an occasion when she had an accident and cut her head badly, she wrote : " Of the two younger ones (if two there were) I have very slight recollections, save that one, a darling child, under five years of age, was quite the pet nursling of the school." This would have been Emily, as Mrs. Gaskell points out, though she was six, not " under five," in September 1824, when she went with Charlotte to Cowan Bridge. Her name was also entered in the School Register with the remark : " Reads very prettily." In Miss Romer Wilson's brilliant but provocative book on Emily Brontë, it is suggested that Emily had a prison complex derived from her sufferings while she was at Cowan Bridge, and that about this time Emily may have been shut up one evening in a dark room at home where she had a fright (as had Jane Eyre when shut up by Mrs. Reed) from the gleam of a passing lamp, whence followed a kind of fit and a vision which haunted her always. It is more probable, going by what " Miss Temple " remembered, that the strong inferiority complex which clouded Emily's life developed when the petting enjoyed at school was put an end to upon the return to Haworth; for at home, between Charlotte, then promoted to the position of " the eldest," and Branwell and Anne, who were very much Aunt's favourites, Emily must often have felt out in the cold.

But all the Brontës must have had abnormal inferiority complexes, physically under-developed, intellectually over-developed children as they were, and living with elders who were constantly in apprehension about something or other, health, cold and damp, risk of fire (one of Mr. Brontë's bugbears) or social dignity, for Mr. Brontë was full of precepts about avoiding slights by taking care not to " outstay one's welcome " if invited anywhere. There can have been little tenderness in their upbringing ; nothing like enough to satisfy ardent, hungry little souls. Papa was severe ; Aunt, partial ; Tabby, kind but sharp. Tenderness was a dream of the past, bound up with memories of Maria and Elizabeth, who were in Heaven now with Mamma, waiting for the others to join them and, meantime, hoping that Charlotte and Branwell and Emily and Anne were being good and growing up to be a comfort to Papa who had so much to bear. The world, early, must have seemed to them a hostile place, and love an almost unattainable ideal. It is easy to see how the themes of " neglected orphan," " mournful boy," " outcast," and " exile," which pervaded their later writings, germinated and developed. Cowper's " Castaway " was a favourite poem of theirs. All of them in turn appropriated its theatrical melancholy :

> *But I beneath a rougher sea*
> *And whelmed in deeper gulfs than he.*

Emily, passionate and intense, but without Charlotte's lust for knowledge and culture, or Anne's awful religious conscience, and up against the fuss made of Branwell, genius as he was thought to be, was soon forced into a silent, defensive "reserve" and early, it seems, became firmly convinced of her unchangeable and bitter fate. Left out of the Angrian game by Charlotte and Branwell, she had to make shift with Anne as a companion, and the family grouping had evidently fallen into these two couples before Charlotte went to school again in 1831, for Charlotte begins a letter from school to Branwell :

" DEAR BRANWELL, – As usual, I address my weekly letter to you because to you I find the most to say."

CHAPTER IV

Charlotte goes to school – Ellen Nussey and Mary Taylor – returns to Angria – Ellen Nussey's picture of the Parsonage group – Charlotte's correspondence with her friends.

IT is the fashion nowadays to laugh at school education, at any rate for geniuses. Miss Romer Wilson, for instance, was highly contemptuous of Charlotte's second excursion into school life in 1831, on the ground that it encouraged her priggishness and zeal for improvement and brought her home, after the year and a half at Miss Wooler's at Roe Head, to administer her scanty bit of book-learning to Emily and Anne – Emily who, says Miss Wilson, " was *hors concours* from the start, unteachable, thank God ! " Such an attitude is all very well for a writer who wants to poetise the Brontës and who gets a romantic pleasure out of depicting them as fated to isolated lives, just as a painter, enamoured of certain atmospheric effects, likes to paint buildings in a place where he can count on their being continuously enveloped in fog. The biographer, however, is not concerned with gloom and isolation for the sake of their romantic effects. It is his job, certainly, to study the twisted psychic developments which go with these surroundings, but not to deplore the intrusion of light or of any commonplace element which, from the painter's or the poet's point of view, robs the situation of its utmost significance. Of course all the Brontës needed a wide, generous education, and would have been the happier for it ; they were fine spirits shut up in a small world – but, their circumstances being what they were, that wide, generous education was not to be had, and Charlotte's little struggle to pick up what schooling she could, and even to hand it on afterwards to her brother and sisters, is not really to be scorned, nor is it pitiable. Going to Roe Head took her outside Haworth, which was a great thing ; it made her friends, Miss Wooler, Mary Taylor and Ellen Nussey, which was even greater – and from the point of view of Brontë lovers, most important, for without the long correspondence which started in school days, amounting to about five hundred letters in all from Charlotte, between Charlotte and Ellen Nussey, very little indeed would be known about the Brontës' home lives.

The first glimpse of Charlotte from the outside comes through her schoolfellow, Mary Taylor, who described to Mrs. Gaskell her arrival at Roe Head School in January 1831 : " I first saw her coming out of a covered cart in very old-fashioned clothes and looking very cold and miserable. She was coming to school at Miss Wooler's. When she appeared in the schoolroom her dress was changed but just as old. She looked a little, old woman, so short-sighted that she always appeared to be seeking something and moving her head from side to side to catch a sight of it. She was very shy and nervous and spoke with a strong Irish accent. When a book was given her, she dropped

Db

her head over it till her nose nearly touched it and when she was told to hold her head up, up went the book after it, still close to her nose so that it was not possible to help laughing."

Ellen Nussey also remembered Charlotte, in the first days at Miss Wooler's, standing by the schoolroom window and crying because of the strangeness. Charlotte was nearly fifteen then : Ellen a year younger. So the two met and became life-long friends.

Charlotte was well read but not well grounded. She knew no grammar and very little geography. "We thought her very ignorant," said Mary Taylor. But it was soon seen that she could quote lots of poetry, and could draw much better than any of them and knew about celebrated pictures and painters ; and though she could not play games (she said she never had played games) and in play-hours always sat or stood with a book, she was a favourite with her school-fellows (not more than ten in all) and in great demand at night as a story-teller of fearsome tales. She was too much in earnest about learning to be thought a prig by her school-fellows, or snubbed because of her passion for improving her mind. "We had a rage for practicality," said Mary Taylor, "and laughed all poetry to scorn." Charlotte, undaunted, went on her solitary way of " picking up every scrap of information concerning painting, sculpture, poetry, music, as if it were gold." The girls, though they teased her and thought her an oddity, championed her. All of them were up in arms once because Charlotte was given a bad mark. She had been set to read a quantity of Blair's *Lectures on Belles-Lettres*, more than she could get through in the time, and she failed to answer some questions on these. The school were furious ; it wasn't fair, they said, to punish Charlotte, who had worked harder than anyone else, and they went on strike in various ways until the bad mark was withdrawn. Charlotte had wept floods over her failure, just as she had wept when, on first going to school, Miss Wooler had told her that until she knew grammar she must be placed in the second class. Miss Wooler's kind heart had been softened, and Charlotte had been put among girls of her own age in the first class and allowed to " catch up " in grammar in her free time.

She was not stand-offish. She was always ready, says Mrs. Gaskell, to try and do what her school-fellows wished, though not sorry when they called her awkward and left her out of their games. Physically, she was feeble and, according to Mary Taylor, " ate no animal food." " Charlotte was never in wild excitement that I know of. When in health she used to talk better and, indeed, when in low spirits, never spoke at all." Mary once told her she was very ugly but repented of it afterwards and said so. Charlotte answered : " You did me a great deal of good, Polly, so don't repent of it." Mary also told her that she and her brother and sisters were like growing potatoes in a cellar. Charlotte said, sadly : " Yes, I know we are." Evidently, she talked to her friends about the others at home, and of the two elder ones, Maria and Elizabeth, who had died. " I used to believe them to have been wonders of talent and kindness," said Mary. She told Mary about the monthly magazine they brought out at home and how they all wrote in it and tried to make it look as like print as possible. She promised, once, to show Mary some copies but then she changed her mind and would not show them. Perhaps she was afraid of Mary laughing at her Wellingtonian heroes, for Mary was a rabid Radical, and at school and at the Taylors' house at Gomersal, Charlotte had to listen to many a diatribe against her cherished parson-bred convictions. At Roe Head she was in the still vivid tracks of Luddite disturbances. Miss Wooler often talked to her pupils of those savage times, of the terrible industrial distress, the bitter, maddened state of the workers, their mysterious, nightly drilling on the moors, their assaults upon mills employing the hated new machinery. Close to Roe Head was Mr. Cartwright's mill, Rawfolds, where a violent attack by hundreds of rioters had been defeated by the coolness and bravery of its owner and a handful of supporters : and at Heckmondwike, a neighbouring village, still lived Parson Roberson, whose fierce but fearless conduct towards the agitators had become a grim legend. Mr. Brontë knew Mr. Roberson ; in some respects they were birds of a feather, and Mr. Helstone of *Shirley* is drawn probably from both of them. Mary Taylor, the Rose Yorke of *Shirley*, wrote to Mrs. Gaskell, when the *Life* was published : " You give much too favourable an

account of the black-coated and Tory savages
that kept the people down and provoked ex-
cesses. . . . Old Roberson said ' he would wade
to the knees in blood rather than the then state of
things should be altered ' – a state including Corn
Law, Test Law and a host of other oppressions."
Mary Taylor, when this was written, was in New
Zealand, whither she had emigrated in 1845,
after family misfortunes. She was a woman of
energy and character and one who never, either
to Charlotte herself or to Charlotte's friends,
minced her opinion that Charlotte's life, from
first to last, was one of sad repression. She would
have liked to see her friend kick over all the traces
and make her own way somehow. " Charlotte,
at school, had no plan of life beyond what circumstances made for her," she wrote to Mrs.
Gaskell and there is, evidently, a criticism in that
remark. Mary herself was essentially rebellious,
more rebellious, probably, than clear-sighted or
possessed of definite aims. Her letters, though
always refreshingly outspoken, show a lack of
something : they start well but often tail off into
inconsequence. It is understandable that, despite
her admiration for Mary's energetic, adventurous
spirit, Charlotte was more drawn to Ellen Nussey
who, though by no means as intelligent as Mary
Taylor, was untroubled by rebellious feelings, and
whose serenity of disposition, combined with
earnest religious beliefs, made her both an example and a prop. Besides, Ellen, a simpler
person altogether than Mary, looked up to Charlotte, whereas Mary just a little looked down on

her. Charlotte could act the schoolmistress to
Ellen ; she could tell her what to read, guide her
tastes. " Your natural abilities are excellent,"
Charlotte wrote to Ellen soon after leaving Roe
Head and back at home again, " and under the
direction of a judicious and able friend . . . you
might acquire a decided taste for elegant literature, and even poetry which, indeed, is included
under that general term. I was very much disappointed by your not sending the hair . . ."
A typical schoolgirls' friendship had started, approached on Charlotte's side with prim, distrust-
ful timidity, born of Papa's precepts. It grew
apace, through letter-writing and visits, and later
became ardent ; indeed, for a time, between 1835
and 1839, Charlotte was near to getting a real
emotional conception, as distinguished from intellectual comprehension, of that hopeless passion
for the Marquis of Douro which had so unhinged
the mind of Lady Zenobia of Angrian fame. But
fiction is one thing and real life another. Charlotte, unlike Lady Zenobia, took a pull at herself
and nipped her passion for Ellen Nussey in the
bud. Ellen Nussey, evidently, did not understand it : she was no Douro and her gentle blue
eyes could never have startled Charlotte with any
look but surprise or mild dismay. However, this
phase of intense feeling, which coincided with a
period of acute religious depression, occurred
after Charlotte's return to Roe Head as a teacher
in July 1835, three years after she had left the
school as a pupil. The intervening three years
were spent at Haworth, teaching her sisters and,

to all outward appearances, resuming the even, but dull, tenor of parsonage life[1]; at the same time, as the mass of Angrian literature written during these years shows, reabsorbed to an extraordinary extent in the imaginary world of her own and Branwell's creation. It was now that Lord Arthur Adrian Augustus Wellesley, Marquis of Douro, Duke of Zamorna began to be the supreme figure (the Duke of Wellington receding into the background whither he emerged at times to preside over family gatherings as in the last scene of *The Spell*), and engaged in deadly political rivalry with Branwell's tool, Percy, Earl of Northangerland, married, it will be remembered, to the terrifying Lady Zenobia. To the astonishing output of this time, Charlotte and Branwell are said to have contributed about equally. Miss Fanny Ratchford, the Brontë Research student of the Wrenn Library, University of Texas, writes in an article in the Publications of the Modern Language Association of America, Vol. XLIII (1928) : " From the very foundation of Verdopolis, Branwell had added his effusions to his sister's, introducing some very interesting, if incongruous elements. It was he who brought revolution and war into Verdopolitan politics and created the

[1] In July 1832, Charlotte wrote from Haworth to Ellen Nussey : "An account of one day is an account of all. In the morning, from nine o'clock till half-past twelve, I instruct my sisters and draw ; then we walk till dinner-time. After dinner, I sew till tea-time, and after tea, I either write, read, or do a little fancy work, or draw, as I please. Thus, in one delightful, though somewhat monotonous, course, my life is spent. I have been out only twice to tea since I came home. We are expecting company this afternoon, and on Tuesday next, we shall have all the female teachers of the Sunday school to tea."

Kingdom of Angria. His contributions, usually wildly imaginative, confused, contradictory and verbose, Charlotte accepted without question and transmuted by her genius into an integral, natural and permanent part of the whole. Indeed, no character, no situation, whether of Charlotte's or Branwell's creation, was ever lost, so easily and naturally did each catch up and use the conception of the other that it is impossible to separate their contributions with certainty." In another draft article which the present writer has been privileged to see, Miss Ratchford says : " Charlotte, during the three years between her schooldays and teaching days at Roe Head, was living a life of golden romance, walking with kings, guiding the destinies of a mighty empire, and receiving the plaudits due to genius from an admiring world," and she goes on to quote secret outpourings written by Charlotte, when at Roe Head again as a teacher, showing what she suffered in exile from Angria and deprived of the excitement of her conjurings with Branwell. The following are extracts :

" Once more, on a dull Saturday afternoon, I sit down to try and summon around me the dim shadows of incidents long departed, of feelings, of pleasures whose exquisite relish I feel it will never be my lot again to taste. How few would believe that from sources purely imaginary such happiness could be derived. Pen cannot portray the deep interests of the scenes . . . I have witnessed in that little room with the low, narrow bed and bare, whitewashed walls, twenty miles away. There have I sat on the low bedstead, my mind fixed on the window through which appeared no other landscape than a monotonous stretch of moorland, a grey church-tower rising from the centre of a churchyard so filled with graves that the rank weeds and coarse grass scarce had room to shoot up between the monuments. . . . Such was the picture that threw its reflection upon my eye but communicated no impression on my heart. . . . A long tale was perhaps evolving itself in my mind, the history of an ancient and aristocratic family . . . young lords and ladies . . . dazzled with the brilliancy of courts, happy with the ambition of senates.

"As I saw them, stately and handsome, gliding through these salons, where many well-known forms crossed my sight, where there were faces looking up, eyes smiling and lips moving in audible speech that I knew better almost than my brother and sisters, yet whose voices never woke an echo in this world. Far from home, I cannot write of them, except in total solitude, I scarce dare think of them."

According to Miss Ratchford, who has studied most of Charlotte's *Juvenilia*, there are many such outpourings, written at Roe Head, all testifying to the same intense absorption in an imaginary world. Haworth itself for its own sake meant little to Charlotte ; it was as the portal of Angria that she pined for it, as the one familiar way to Verdopolis. The landscape to be seen from the Parsonage windows, and the winds which howled round the Parsonage walls, were, so to speak, the keys of her secret Heaven.

" That wind," she wrote, " pouring in impetuous currents through the air, sounding wildly, un-
remittingly from hour to hour, deepening its tone
as the night advances, coming, not in gusts but
with a rapid gathering, stormy swell—that wind,
I know, is heard at this moment far away on the
moors of Haworth. Branwell and Emily hear it,
and as it sweeps over our house down the churchyard and round the old church they think perhaps, of me and Anne." (Anne was then with
Charlotte at Roe Head.) " Glorious that blast
was, mighty ; it reminded me of Northangerland ; there was something so merciless in the
heavier rush that made the very house groan as if
it could scarce bear this acceleration of impulse."

Again : " I listened—the sound sailed full and
liquid . . . the bells of Huddersfield Parish Church.
I shut the window and went back to my seat. Then
came on me, rushing impetuously, all the mighty
phantasm that this had conjured from nothing—
from nothing to a system strange as some religious
creed. I felt as if I could have written gloriously.
The spirit of all Verdopolis, of all the mountain-
ous North, of all the woodland West, of all the
river watered East, came crowding into my mind.
If I had had time to indulge it, I felt that the vague
suggestions of that moment would have settled
down into some narrative better at least than anything I ever produced before. But just then a dolt
came up with a lesson . . ."

It certainly seems extraordinary, even a little
uncanny, this intense, persistent absorption on a
girl's part in an unreal world. The persistence, of

course, must have been, to some extent, deliberate. Charlotte was determined not to be parted from Angrian splendours and palaces : she resented the intrusion of the commonplace, the dolt, for instance, who came up for a lesson and broke into her day-dreams. There is a note of self-conscious pride in her remark : " How few would believe that from sources purely imaginary such happiness can be derived " ; and even a little swagger in her reference to that " mighty phantasm . . . strange as some religious creed." The company at Roe Head were not, in fact, any more than was the society at Haworth, drawn from the class with whom Charlotte, in her fancies, had been accustomed to mix. Her attitude was not unlike that of Aunt Branwell who sat upstairs in her bedroom, bemoaning the cold of the downstairs regions, and harping on the charms of far-away Penzance. It seems an unkind thing to say of timid, shrinking little Charlotte Brontë that at bottom she had too exalted an opinion of herself, and of course it cannot be said without explaining that by exalted opinion is meant, in the main, an exaggerated sense of self-importance due to repression in childish days and lack of normal contacts. This was largely the matter with all the Brontës (though possibly there is something also to be said for the contention that consciously they thought themselves a bit above their neighbours) ; their wretched shyness arose from it, as most shyness does, and, open expression of self-importance being denied them by circumstance and precept, indirect " symbolic " expression was an inevitable result. Moreover, day-dreaming in Angria was almost Charlotte's only relaxation. Most young people have a variety of amusements, outdoor games and exercises, parties, etc. ; Charlotte had but one game. This fact strengthened the game's grip upon her imagination, gave the doings of her Angrian grandees a continuity in her mind, put them in sole possession of her leisure hours. Writing about them made them of still greater consequence. A reader can put a book down and forget about the story in it. The play ends when the curtain falls. But in the writer's mind, the curtain never falls. The story goes on ; the characters live and struggle and suffer all the time. They are bone of the writer's bone and flesh of his flesh, even though he may not always be able to communicate their reality to the reader. Indeed, in that case, they may live in the writer's mind even more insistently, clamouring to be more fully realised, to be, as it were, *born*. Few of Charlotte's heroes ever were born, though they lived with her for a life-time. Douro became Mr. Rochester in *Jane Eyre*, but still remained an unreal figure. Of the chief personages in that book only Jane Eyre herself came to life and lived on in Lucy Snowe in *Villette*.

Yet, despite Angria, despite the monotonous daily round at Haworth, Charlotte's life was altering. She was ceasing to be a child able to satisfy herself with make-believe. The sense of exile she felt during her second stay at Roe Head might have overcome her at home. Even there, the old familiar surroundings might have failed, at times, to open the Angrian doors. Charlotte was growing up ; her brother and sisters were growing up. Branwell's future was beginning to be in question ; the future of the girls too, in a lesser degree.

We get a picture, the only one of the family as a whole, from Ellen Nussey, who paid a return visit at the Parsonage in the summer of 1833. Charlotte had visited Ellen at the Rydings, Birstall, in the previous September.

Ellen Nussey wrote, in her *Reminiscences* : " My first visit to Haworth was full of novelty and freshness. The scenery for some miles before we reached Haworth was wild and uncultivated . . . at last, we came to what seemed a terrific hill, such a deep declivity no one thought of riding down it ; the horse had to be carefully led. We no sooner reached the foot of this hill than we had to begin to mount again, over a narrow, rough, stonepaved road. . . . When we reached the top of the village, there was apparently no outlet, but we were directed to drive into an entry which just admitted the gig ; we wound round in this entry and then saw the church close at hand, and we entered on the short lane which led to the parsonage gateway. Here Charlotte was waiting, having caught the sound of the approaching gig. When greetings and introductions were over, Miss Branwell . . . took possession of their guest and treated her with the care and solicitude due to a weary traveller. Mr. Brontë, also, was stirred out of his usual retirement by his own kind consideration, for not only the guest but the man-servant and the horse were to be made comfortable. . . .

Even at this time, Mr. Brontë struck me as looking very venerable, with his snow-white hair
and powdered coat-collar. His manner and
mode of speech always had the tone of highbred
courtesy. He was considered somewhat of an in-
valid and always lived in the most abstemious and
simple manner. His white cravat was not then
so remarkable as it grew to be afterwards. He
was in the habit of covering this cravat himself.
We never saw the operation but we always had to
wind for him the white sewing-silk which he used.
Charlotte said it was her father's one extravagance
– he cut up yards and yards of white lute-string
(silk) in covering his cravat and . . . went into new
silk and new size without taking any off, till at
length nearly half his head was enveloped in
cravat. His liability to bronchial attacks, no
doubt, attached him to this increasing growth of
cravat.

"Miss Branwell . . . was a small, antiquated little
lady. She wore caps large enough for half a
dozen of the present fashion and a front of light
auburn curls over her forehead. She always
dressed in silk. She had a horror of the climate
so far north, and of the stone floors of the parsonage. She amused us by clicking about in
pattens whenever she had to go into the kitchen or
look after household operations.

"She talked a great deal of her younger days : the
gaieties of her native town, Penzance ; the soft,
warm climate. The social life of her younger
days she used to recall with regret ; she gave one
the idea that she had been a belle among her own

home acquaintances. She took snuff out of a very pretty gold snuff-box which she sometimes presented to you with a little laugh, as if she enjoyed the slight shock and astonishment visible in your countenance. In summer, she spent part of the afternoon in reading aloud to Mr. Brontë. In the winter evenings, she must have enjoyed this ; for she and Mr. Brontë had often to finish their discussions on what she had read when we all met for tea. She would be very lively and intelligent and tilt arguments against Mr. Brontë without fear.

" ' Tabby,' the faithful, trustworthy old servant was very quaint in appearance – very active and, in these days, the general servant and factotum. We were all ' childer ' and ' bairns ' in her estimation. She still kept to her duty of walking out with the ' childer,' if they went any distance from home, unless Branwell were sent by his father as a protector.

" Emily Brontë had by this time acquired a lithesome, graceful figure. She was the tallest person in the house, except her father. Her hair, which was naturally as beautiful as Charlotte's, was in the same unbecoming tight curl and frizz and there was the same want of complexion. She had very beautiful eyes – kind, kindling, liquid eyes ; but she did not often look at you ; she was too reserved. Their colour might be said to be dark grey, at other times dark blue, they varied so. She talked very little. She and Anne were like twins – inseparable companions, and in the very closest sympathy which never had any interruption.

" Anne – dear, gentle Anne – was quite different

in appearance from the others. She was her
aunt's favourite. Her hair was a very pretty light
brown and fell on her neck in graceful curls. She
had lovely violet-blue eyes, fine, pencilled eye-
brows, and clear, almost transparent complexion.
She still pursued her studies, and especially her sewing, under the surveillance of her aunt. Emily had
now begun to have the disposal of her own time.

" Branwell studied regularly with his father and
used to paint in oils, which was regarded as study
for what might be eventually his profession. All the
household entertained the idea of his becoming an
artist and hoped he would be a distinguished one.

" In fine and suitable weather delightful
rambles were made over the moors and down
into glens and ravines that here and there broke
the monotony of the moorland. The rugged
bank and rippling brook were treasures of delight.
Emily, Anne and Branwell used to ford the
streams, and sometimes placed stepping-stones
for the other two. There was always a lingering
delight in these sports – every moss, every flower,
every tint and form, were noted and enjoyed.
Emily, especially, had a gleesome delight in these
nooks of beauty – her reserve for the time
vanished. One long ramble made in these early
days was far away over the moors, to a spot
familiar to Emily and Anne which they called
' The Meeting of the Waters.' It was a small
oasis of emerald green turf, broken here and there
by small clear springs ; a few large stones served
as resting-places ; seated here, we were hidden
from all the world, nothing appearing in view but

miles and miles of heather, a glorious blue sky and brightening sun. A fresh breeze wafted on us its exhilarating influence ; we laughed and made mirth of each other, and settled we would call ourselves the quartette. Emily, half reclining on a slab of stone, played like a young child with the tadpoles in the water, making them swim about, and then fell to moralising on the strong and the weak, the brave and the cowardly, as she chased them with her hand.

" The interior of the now far-famed parsonage lacked drapery of all kinds. Mr. Brontë's horror of fire forbade curtains to the windows . . . there was not much carpet anywhere except in the sitting-room and on the study floor. The hall floor and stairs were done with sandstone, always beautifully clean, as everything was about the house ; the walls were not papered, but stained in a pretty dove-coloured tint ; hair-seated chairs and mahogany tables, bookshelves in the study, but not many of these elsewhere. Scant and bare indeed, many will say, yet it was not a scantness that made itself felt. Mind and thought, I had almost said elegance, but certainly refinement, diffused themselves over all, and made nothing really wanting."

This is a vivid picture. Brontë lovers would be poor without it, indeed without it could hardly set eyes on the Parsonage group. How clearly we can see them all upon " Miss " Nussey's arrival : Charlotte waiting for her friend in the lane ; Mr. Brontë, venerable-looking at fifty-five, his neck swathed in that huge choker, emerging

Eb

from his study to greet the visitor ; little, old-
fashioned Miss Branwell rustling forward to do
the honours ; silent, lanky Emily and shy Anne,
not daring to be absent on this great occasion but
very loth to be noticed, linked together in the
background. Mr. Brontë and Miss Branwell, no
doubt, did most of the talking at tea for Miss
Nussey's benefit, until Branwell came in, small,
red-haired, spectacled and talkative, his father's
pride and his aunt's pet. Not a word, we may
be sure, came from Emily or Anne unless they
were spoken to, and as soon as they could, these
" inseparables " would have disappeared. Emily,
Miss Nussey observed, was the tallest of the family,
except her father, which observation has led many
people to suppose that she was very tall. But her
full-grown height was not more than five feet six
inches, as her coffin measurements show. Charlotte was short, though not a dwarf, as Miss
Martineau suggested when she described Charlotte as the smallest person she had ever seen outside a fair ; she was five feet two inches. Anne
and Branwell were also short.

The visit was a great success. Miss Nussey was
highly approved of by all, including Tabby, who
did not take to everyone, by any means. Charlotte's letters to Ellen reported this : " Papa and
Aunt are continually adducing you as an example
for me . . . Emily and Anne say ' they never saw
anyone they liked so well as Miss Nussey ' " – and
the correspondence went on. Charlotte used
Ellen as a dumping-ground for home-manu-
factured sententiousness and wrote to her as if she

were an elderly aunt – " What a remarkable winter we have had ! Rain and wind continually but an almost total absence of frost and snow " – and continued the task of cultivating Ellen's taste for elegant literature, winding up a disquisition by the remark – " adhere to standard authors and avoid novelty."

Ellen, whether she profited or not, kept all Charlotte's letters, which is more than Mary Taylor, to whom Charlotte also wrote occasionally, did ; this is a loss for the biographer for it would have been interesting to compare the two sets of letters and to see whether Charlotte was essentially didactic or whether the elderly aunt strain was brought out of her by Ellen's admiration for her clever friend. Evidently, however, Charlotte held forth on politics when she wrote to Mary. " Brougham, you see, is triumphant. Wretch ! I am a hearty hater, and if there is anyone I thoroughly abhor, it is that man." She writes this to Ellen and then remarks that Ellen has brought this rodomontade on herself by telling her to write as she writes to Mary Taylor. Mary was stony ground, as far as reclamation to Tory principles was concerned ; but still, for all her fiery Radicalism, her letters were worth having and, on paper, Charlotte loved crossing swords. There was no " kick " to be got out of Ellen, but, all the same, Charlotte loved her best. " In the solitude of our wild little hill village," wrote Charlotte to her, "I think of my only unrelated friend – my dear, *ci-devant* school-companion, daily, nay almost hourly." " Farewell, *dearest, dearest.*"

CHAPTER V

MR. BRONTË's stipend was about £200 a year. Though he lived rent free and wages were low, there could not have been much to spare for education. Mr. Brontë was " both liberal and charitable," Mrs. Gaskell says, and he sent money from time to time to his Irish relations. Nevertheless, large families were brought up on incomes of this size in those days, families whom it would be an exaggeration to call " poverty-stricken," unless that word is used to describe all those who have very little left after providing for necessaries. The school fees for the four children at Cowan Bridge amounted to about £60 a year, and though relations and friends may have helped with this payment, Mr. Brontë was evidently prepared to squeeze something out of his income for education, or Branwell's career as a painter would not have been contemplated.

The expenses of training Branwell do not, however, seem to have been considered carefully. " Branwell is going to London," Charlotte tells Ellen in a letter (July 1835) in which she writes that she is returning to Roe Head as a teacher and that Emily is going with her as a pupil. There is an undated letter from Branwell to the

Secretary of the Royal Academy, announcing his
" earnest desire to enter as a probationary
student " there and asking when he ought to present his drawings, in order to qualify for entrance ;
but there is no evidence of his admission or that
he ever entered for the preliminary examination.
He certainly went to London and he saw some
of the " sights," but he soon returned to Haworth,
presumably having concluded that an artist's
career in London was beyond him, having regard
to his lack of training and the time and expense
that studentship at the Royal Academy would
have involved. He had no training beyond
lessons in portrait painting from a Leeds painter,
William Robinson ; it is not surprising that his
work had no technical merit. The well-known
specimens of it – the portraits of his sisters, now
in the National Portrait Gallery – seem to show
a power of bringing out character, but it may be
the very crudity of the painting which gives that
impression to searching eyes. From boyhood he
had had great fondness for drawing, as had also
his sisters – Charlotte strained her sight seriously
by prolonged efforts to produce exact copies of
old engravings – and all at one time had drawing
lessons from Mr. Robinson. When Ellen Nussey
paid her first visit to Haworth, Branwell, then
aged sixteen, was painting in oils and the family
appear to have taken for granted that he would
succeed as a painter. He never came near success
as everyone knows, but as few would have known
or been concerned to enquire about, if Mrs.
Gaskell, and other writers who took their cue

from her, had not very much exaggerated the period of Branwell's downfall and dissipation, dating it almost from the London visit and making it a kind of Rake's Progress from then onwards.

Branwell's story is one of almost everyday occurrence, the story of a brilliant, charming boy, the pride and hope of his family, the delight of his friends, who failed to satisfy that hope, partly because it was excessive and the means of realising it were lacking, and partly because of the psychic injury inflicted upon anyone from whom from childhood onwards too much is expected and upon whom too much advance admiration is lavished. Branwell was the "show" youth of Haworth; the "draw" to visitors at the "Black Bull," whose landlord was ready enough that he should make himself at home there. Notice and conviviality were pleasant to him, as they are to most young people, and the easy friendliness of the inn and other village institutions must have been sweet to a boy escaping from solitary work in his father's study and the puritanical atmosphere of home. The world, when Branwell adventured into it, excitable, self-confident at times to an absurd degree, as his letters to the editor of *Blackwood's Magazine* show, but at other times despondent and given to religious gloom, did not take his genius for granted, as Haworth did, but still, to the enthusiastic boy, it glittered. Good company and popularity were to be had for little more than the exercise of his ready wit and versatile imagination. Strong will power and resolution are needed, at any age, to put the necessity of earning a living before social pleasures and longings for a life of the mind, and, untrained as Branwell was for a profession, the livelihoods open to him were not such as could yield much, if indeed any, intellectual interest. Small wonder then that, after a vain attempt to make a living by portrait painting in Bradford, he had a succession of jobs, as had also his sister, Charlotte, for which by temperament and upbringing he was, like her, utterly unsuited, and that, in the intervals between and leisure during these uncongenial employments, he sought lively company and often drank more than was good for him. He certainly idled as a clerk at Luddenden Foot, then a remote country railway station where, in between the passing of trains, there was little to be done and where, except for an occasional visit from a crony, Branwell sat alone in a wooden shanty amusing himself now and again by scribbling sketches on the margins of railway account books. But he gave satisfaction in his tutorial posts and did not go to pieces until his last situation, from which he was dismissed because, having fallen madly and hopelessly in love with his employer's wife, he completely lost his self-control and became obsessed by his passion. Then, and not until then (1844, at the earliest), can Branwell's collapse justly be said to have started ; his history during the previous years being disappointing only to those, including himself, who had thoughtlessly believed that his particular abilities would carry him to success without training or social backing, and who had never, apparently, considered that those

same abilities might be a grave drawback to him
in seeking or keeping to the dull round of ordinary,
unintellectual employment.

The experiment of sending Emily with Charlotte when the latter returned to Roe Head as a
teacher was, as Emily herself might have said,
" no go." Charlotte gave an account of it in that
well-known passage in the memoir of her sisters,
telling how Emily became so ill from homesickness that she had to be sent back to Haworth after
three months of school. Charlotte, who stayed
on with Anne, who took Emily's place, was also
miserably homesick, for Angria, as we now know.
Emily's homesickness may have been for Gondal-
land, or its predecessor ; we have only Charlotte's
word for it that it was the moors for which she
pined. Emily was far more secretive even than
Charlotte about her inmost feelings and Charlotte
never mentioned Angria when she wrote to Ellen
saying how wretched she was. Charlotte gave
Ellen to suppose that she was in the depths of
religious despondency which could only be
allayed by the companionship of Ellen ; she also
made it clear that she loathed teaching. Just as
she kept her Angrian dreams from Ellen and from
everyone except perhaps Branwell, who still seems
to have been engaged, wherever he was, in com-
passing Zamorna's downfall,[1] so, even if she knew

[1] Charlotte's secret outpourings at Roe Head contain the
following diary notes :
" About a week since, I got a letter from Branwell containing
a most exquisitely characteristic epistle from Northangerland to
his daughter . . . I lived on its contents for days " ; and
" I wonder if Branwell has really killed the Duchess. Is she
dead ? Is she buried ? Is she alone in the cold earth on this

what Emily was brooding over, she was not likely to have told. But, probably, she did not know and homesickness for the moors was as near as she could get towards explaining what was the matter with Emily.

"My sister Emily loved the moors," wrote Charlotte. True as that was, of course it was not the whole truth. We do not, nowadays, make Mrs. Gaskell's mistake of supposing that Emily cared only for nature and animals. The attraction which has been felt towards her of late years is as much an understanding of the passionate nature that was behind that seeming coldness of hers as it is due to appreciation of her as a writer and poet. The Victorian predilection for lives of valiant souls "made perfect by suffering," to quote from a letter Charles Kingsley wrote to Mrs. Gaskell, has yielded to a sympathetic interest in the psychology of human beings regardless of whether suffering makes them perfect or not. When Mrs. Gaskell was writing her life of Charlotte, she asked Ellen Nussey what Emily's religious opinions were. Miss Nussey, a devout Churchwoman, was not at all certain and to Mrs. Gaskell, Unitarian and wide-minded as she was, this uncertainty evidently constituted a serious obstacle to knowledge of Emily, of whom, from talks with various people, she had already formed no very pleasant impression.

Mrs. Gaskell's impression was, no doubt,

dreary night? . . . Her removal, if it has taken place, must have been to Northangerland like the quenching of the last spark that averted utter darkness."

correct. Emily's *farouche* reserve and self-will
could not have made her an agreeable person.
Outside her family, she had no personal friends ;
only a few people knew her even superficially ;
most of those of her own social standing who came
in contact with her found her most difficult to get
on with.[1] That towards humbler folk like the
Haworth villagers she was unalarming, kind and
even genial at times, as Mme. Duclaux records,
is quite compatible with the story of her disagree-
ableness. Where no fear of intrusion upon her
inner self threatened, she could be at ease. So,
with Anne, and with anyone or anything turning
to her for protection, she was devotion itself, giving
loving companionship, unselfishness, sympathy,
everything, in short, with which natures like
Emily's are so often endowed, except those ulti-
mate, inmost confidences which some innate fear
forbade her ever giving. Fear of what, she could
not probably have told, but it must have been
something which made community of thought
and feeling a terror to her and turned the idea of
friendship into a sort of threat.

There seems no need to search for some particular psychological disturbance, issuing from a
fit or a shock in childhood, to account for the
almost sterilising fear which isolated Emily
Brontë from so much in life that she needed,
needed as much as the light and air and expanses
of her moors. " The cliverest o' the Brontës," so

[1] In 1924, Sir Clifford Allbutt wrote to the late Sir Edmund
Gosse :
" It was not Charlotte who was ' gey ill to live with ' but *Emily*.
No human being . . . could get on with Emily Brontë."

they spoke of her in the village, " the genius of the family," as in old age, Mr. Brontë once admitted to a visitor, that he considered her to have been, may have come by her fierce and excessive reserve out of sub-conscious jealousy of Branwell who, as the only son, received all the attention, and of Charlotte who, as the eldest, ordered the others about. Her poems around the " mournful boy " theme, as Miss Romer Wilson has insisted, all point to that recurring idea of herself as a friendless, unwanted child cast into an alien world –

> *I am the only being whose doom*
> *No tongue would ask, no eye would mourn –*

and the attraction which orphans and castaways had for all the Brontë children resolved itself, in her case, into that passion for the *âme damnée* which came to fullest expression in the creation of Heathcliff in *Wuthering Heights*.

It seems, however, a mistake to represent Emily as within the conscious heart of her at enmity with mankind. She was evidently a proud, deepnatured, loving and undemonstrative person, bent on her own way, but that way was a simple straightforward one, directed not so much against the world as away from conventional bounds and restrictions. Freedom was the breath of her soul ; and to get that, and to be relieved from the odious necessity of becoming a governess, she willingly undertook at home domestic duties far less irksome to her than looking after tiresome children and being boxed up with strangers. There were times when she wished the Parsonage and monotonous daily work at Jericho and then she rushed out on to the moors. The moors soothed her and gave her a sense of infinity which she loved because life at home and in the village was cramped and small. They gave her joy too, of an ecstatic kind, different from the dreary comfort that was preached and sung in church. She could stretch her limbs on the moors ; she could pretend there to be the boy she often wished she had been born. There were no critical eyes upon her there ; only now and again she might meet a farm-hand or a shawled woman and be the cheerier for a greeting with them. The moor folk, the Haworth villagers going about their daily work, were the kind of people she liked to see and all the society she thought she wanted. It wasn't irksome to be on friendly terms with them. It was flattering and, better still, satisfying to be liked by them ; there is a sort of sacramental pleasure in easy contact with simple folk, the sacrament of common, divine friendliness which asks for nothing back and knows no disappointments or regrets and might, it would seem, be celebrated all the year long over the whole earth, only somehow there must be difficulties because it certainly isn't ! Generally, people want more : that is the trouble. Emily too wanted more, sometimes, from someone, from somewhere . . . the moors weren't really enough. At times, she was desperately lonely.

So home she came, after the three months at Roe Head, and there she stayed for about two

years when another short-lived attempt was made
to launch her into school. She went as a governess to a large school at Law Hill, near Halifax,
where, from an account she gave of it to Charlotte
which was retailed to Ellen, she was kept at work
" from six in the morning until near eleven at
night." Charlotte seems to have forgotten this
episode for, in the memoir before mentioned, she
writes as if Emily never left home again after Roe
Head until the two of them went to Brussels together in 1842. Either Charlotte had a bad
memory for dates and events or, when writing
the memoir (which has another inaccuracy in it
besides this one), she purposely left out what did
not fit in with the picture of Emily she was then
drawing.

Nothing else is known of Emily's time at Law
Hill, though it has been suggested that she
obtained " colour " there for *Wuthering Heights*.
Mme. Duclaux, probably told by Miss Nussey,
says that Emily endured the school for a couple of
terms and then gave it up. Charlotte, in the
meantime, was at Dewsbury Moor, whither Miss
Wooler's school had removed from Roe Head, disliking the place and disliking her job more and
more, and outpouring to Ellen, who was out of
reach, paying visits and, Charlotte feared, for-
getting her, that her heart was a " real hot-bed
of sinful thoughts." Miss Wooler was kind, but
Charlotte hated teaching (which, in those days,
seems to have included doing the pupils' mending
as well) and as she was terribly conscientious and
could only be got with difficulty to take outings

and visit friends in the neighbourhood, she worked herself up into a very morbid and irritable condition, feeling a lost soul and (what was really the matter) feeling unloved. At Christmas, 1837, she had a " scene " with Miss Wooler, ostensibly over Anne's health, but really over the pathetic self-importance of Charlotte who was aching for regard and praise. Miss Wooler did the tactful thing and said how sorry she would be to lose her, so Charlotte, who had previously decided to leave, said she would stay. Charlotte was quite aware of her " touchiness " ; in a later letter to Ellen, she wrote : " If I made you my Father Confessor, I could reveal weaknesses which you do not dream of. I do not mean to intimate that I attach a *high value* to empty compliments but a word of panegyric has often made me feel a sense of confused pleasure which it required my strongest efforts to conceal – and, on the other hand, a hasty expression which I could construe into neglect or disapprobation has tortured me till I have lost half a night's rest from its rankling pangs." How much happier she would have been if she had not used her strongest efforts to conceal her enjoyment of " panegyric " ; but Charlotte's whole life was a battle between natural longings and censure of them by the rules of conduct in which she had been brought up.

Charlotte, however, did not stay much longer at Dewsbury Moor. She became more morbid, her health suffered, and a doctor whom she consulted advised her to go home. Loathing of the work, excess of conscience masking all kinds of

ambitions, to write, and see her name in print, to
be celebrated, beautiful, popular and affluent, to
be anything but a poor, plain little governess,
were at the bottom of her neurotic state ; there
is no need to look further afield to discover why
she afterwards spoke of Dewsbury Moor as a
"poisonous place." Back at home she felt
better ; the Taylors came to stay that summer,
and she went later to stay with her "darling
Ellen." In the following spring (1839) Ellen's
brother, Henry, a very proper but cold-blooded
young curate, made Charlotte an offer of marriage. Charlotte sat down at once and penned a
long "decided negative." Afterwards, she un-
burdened herself to Ellen of the "strong temptation" which the proposal had held. "I thought
if I were to marry Henry Nussey, his sister could
live with me." However, consideration for
Henry's happiness disposed of the temptation
and Charlotte admitted she had felt bound to
think of herself as well. "If ever I marry, it must
be in the light of adoration that I will regard my
husband." "Ten to one, I shall never have the
chance again, but *n'importe*," she added, gaily.
Mr. Nussey's offer, though unacceptable, had done
her good. She left home again, a couple of months
later, to be governess to the Sidgwicks at Stonegappe, near Skipton, in a cheerful mood, but the
new situation was no more bearable than the last
had been. Charlotte was not made to be a
governess. She did not "understand children,"
but as parents and other sentimental people invariably say this of those who speak frankly of

their darlings, it is not necessary to assume that the Sidgwick children, even when understood, were a pleasure to teach. Mr. A. C. Benson admits that his cousin, " Benson Sidgwick, now vicar of Ashby Parva," certainly on one occasion threw a Bible at Miss Brontë, and seems to suggest that Miss Brontë need not have minded that. However, as Charlotte did not then know that Benson Sidgwick would one day be a vicar, she probably did mind. At any rate, she described the Sidgwicks as " riotous, perverse, unmanageable cubs," " pampered, spoiled and turbulent, whom I was expected constantly to amuse as well as to instruct."

Poor Charlotte! Many things were expected of her (sewing and mending in abundance) and, unfortunately, she expected things of her employers that were not, under the circumstances, to be obtained. She expected that Mrs. Sidgwick should understand her, but governesses were just governesses in those days, there to do their duty and not to be understood. Charlotte's " stock of animal spirits," never worth mentioning, sank very low. Mrs. Sidgwick took her to task about her depression and Charlotte cried bitterly ; it all seemed so unkind. " Mrs. Sidgwick's health is sound – her animal spirits are good – consequently she is cheerful in company," Charlotte moaned to Ellen ; but how could it be expected that she, Charlotte, could be cheerful in such a place ? She left it after three months. The Brontës could always be trusted to leave their situations. Except, perhaps, Anne. She, good,

mild girl, far shyer than Charlotte, but with a
sense of humour which Charlotte lacked, was
wrestling with the young Inghams at Blake Hall –
" an unruly, violent family of modern children,"
so Charlotte, from Anne's letters, summed them
up. Anne bore with them until Christmas (1839);
it was then decided, probably by Charlotte, that
Anne was not to return. But she stayed over four
years in her last post with the Robinsons at Thorp
Green – a Brontë record !

Charlotte remained at home for nearly two
years before she found another situation. A good
deal happened during that time. She went for a
month to the seaside with Ellen and sobbed at her
first sight of the sea. She received a second offer
of marriage, from a young Irish curate who was
brought to the Parsonage by his vicar to spend the
day. Charlotte had evidently made herself most
agreeable – " at home, you know, Ellen, I talk
with ease and am never shy " – and Mr. Bryce
and she had laughed and joked together until she
noticed some " Hibernian flattery " in his conversation that she did not " relish." A few days
later came an ardent love letter and proposal, at
which Charlotte laughed. Six months later, the
impulsive youth died suddenly : the news gave
the might-have-been widow quite a shock. The
great excitement, however, was the arrival of a
curate at Haworth, Mr. Brontë's eyesight having
begun to fail. This young man, William Weightman, nicknamed " Celia Amelia " by the Parsonage girls because of his pink and white beauty,
soon became a great attraction. Charlotte, of

Fʙ

course, pretended to be indifferent and, later, contemptuous, but it is clear, from the room he takes up in her letters to Ellen, that at first, at any rate, she was thrilled by him. She drew his portrait and the sittings, Miss Nussey says, became alarmingly long. Anne, on her holidays, fell in love with Willie Weightman. Even Emily relaxed. He was said to have been the only curate she ever tolerated, her usual behaviour on entering a room and finding a curate there being to go away at once.

" Celia Amelia " brought life and fun into the Parsonage. He teased " Aunt " and sent the girls valentines. But it was soon seen – at least so Charlotte declared – that he was an outrageous flirt, and not to be taken seriously. Charlotte told the tale of his numerous victims to Ellen who, herself, had been smitten, but, kept regularly posted as to his fickleness, was prevented from cherishing hopes. Ellen, moreover, was considering another possible suitor who, apparently, never came to the point. Charlotte was busy for some time in her old rôle of elderly aunt, advising Ellen to take Mr. Vincent if he should propose, despite not being exactly keen about him. " My good girl, *une grande passion* is *une grande folie*. Is the man a fool, a knave, a humbug, a hypocrite, a ninny, a noodle ? If he is any or all of these, of course there is no sense in trifling with him. . . . Is he something better than this ? Has he common sense, a good disposition, a manageable temper ? Then, Nell, consider the matter. . . ." " No young lady should fall in

love till the offer has been made, accepted, the
marriage ceremony performed, and the first half
year of wedded life has passed away. A woman
may then begin to love, but with great precau-
tion, very coolly, very moderately, very ration-
ally. . . ." Either Charlotte had burnt her
fingers, or she was spouting from some of the
French novels the Taylors had lately lent her –
and fancied herself as an aged cynic.

A masculine jauntiness had begun to mark her
letters, and continued. This may have been partly
the influence of Branwell, who was at home during
the summer of 1840, in between leaving a tutor's
post and starting as a railway clerk. He affected
a *blasé*, Don Juan manner of writing ; indeed, the
famous " Old Knave of Trumps " letter, written
by him to a personal friend and brother-mason,
the Master of the Haworth Lodge of the Three
Graces, which has so often been held up as evidence of Branwell's shocking depravity, is no
more than a specimen of a young man's aping of
fashionable *diablerie*, and there are passages in one
or two of Charlotte's letters to Ellen not very
different in their affectation of a bold hardihood.
The Marquis of Douro's insolent shade was still
hovering in the background, and just as Branwell
liked to pretend to John Brown and his brother
that he was a bit of a dog, so Charlotte occasionally fancied herself as a knowing bird, not to be
caught by Willie Weightman's triflings, or to be
taken in by any sentimentalism. She had given
up writing poetry, so she told Henry Nussey to
whom she wrote worldly-wise letters from time to

time. She was looking out for another post which she found, early in 1841, with the Whites of Upperwood House, Rawdon. "This place is far better than Stonegappe, but God knows I have enough to do to keep a good heart in the matter," she wrote. "The children are not such little devils incarnate as the Sidgwicks but they are over-indulged and at times hard to manage." The Whites were evidently kind to Charlotte ; despite their " low extraction," she admitted it. They invited Mr. Brontë to stay for a week. Charlotte writhed : " it would be like incurring an obligation." She was longing to escape, and a letter from Mary Taylor, in August, full of a tour on the Continent, gave her a *mauvais quart d'heure*. A plan had been mooted at home during the summer holidays of her starting a school with Emily and Anne. " Aunt " had actually intimated that she might lend £150 for the purpose. Various plans were suggested, among them a suggestion of Miss Wooler's, that the Dewsbury Moor School should be taken over by the Brontës. But Charlotte had another scheme by this time, encouraged by Mary Taylor. This was to go to Brussels, to learn French thoroughly and pick up German before starting a school herself. Visions of cathedrals and picture galleries such as Mary had seen came before her and wings seemed to be growing out of her shoulder blades.

Emily was to go too : what she felt about it is not known. She apparently approved of the first plan for setting up a school. The two notes,

written by her and Anne on Emily's birthday,
July 30th, 1841, to be opened four years later,
refer to the plan hopefully and Emily is interested
enough for part of her note to be taken up with
anticipating the future if the plan should ma-
terialise. " This day four years I wonder if we
shall still be dragging on in our present condition
or established to our hearts' content. I guess that
at the time appointed for the opening of this paper
we . . . shall be all merrily seated in our own
sitting-room in some pleasant and flourishing
seminary. . . . It will be a fine warm summer
evening very different from this bleak look-
out. . . ." " This bleak look-out " was the view
from Haworth dining-room where Emily was sitting writing her note. Both notes, though Anne's
less than Emily's, show that childish habit,
noticed in one of Charlotte's early chronicles,
of starting to write by putting down the exact
whereabouts of other members of the family.
Emily begins : " I am seated in the dining-room,
having just concluded tidying our desk boxes . . .
Papa is in the parlour – Aunt upstairs in her room.
Keeper is in the kitchen – Hero in his cage . . ."
One wonders if this almost geographical exacti-
tude was deliberate in order that four years later
the sisters should be able to see the past scene, or
whether it came from an unusual precision in the
Brontë make-up. Or was it just the Brontës' way,
Emily's especially, of coming down to earth for
practical purposes, living as they did so much in
an imaginary world ?

The Gondal-land *finale* of the notes together

with the reference to " dragging on " and " this bleak look-out," suggest that Emily did not idealise Haworth, and Charlotte's excitement at the thought of going abroad may, for the time being, have overcome Emily's horror of going among strangers and into a foreign world. The Brussels school was decided upon – Aunt advanced the money for fees – and in February 1842, escorted by their father, Charlotte and Emily arrived at the Pensionnat Héger, Rue d'Isabelle.

CHAPTER VI

THE externals, at any rate, of the Brontës' life in Brussels have been depicted in Charlotte's two novels, *The Professor* and *Villette*. Until 1894, when the Héger Pensionnat in the Rue d'Isabelle was pulled down, it was possible, with these books as a guide, to find one's way through the former schoolrooms and dormitories and to identify the neighbouring *Athénée* and the small window in it overlooking the Pensionnat garden and the *allée défendue*. If there were any doubt (which, apparently, according to those who knew the Hégers, there is not) as to the originals of M. Paul Emanuel and Mme. Beck in *Villette*, Charlotte's anxiety to prevent a French edition of the book from appearing would dispose of it.

The Brontës were not happy in Brussels. It was hardly to be expected that they would be. They were past the school-girl age – Charlotte was nearly twenty-six, Emily twenty-three-and-a-half – when they arrived there. They were Protestant to the core and Charlotte, despite her enthusiasm for travel and the sight of foreign places, was not unlike M. Taine's Englishwoman who, on reaching Paris, wrote home saying :

"There are so many foreigners here." Brussels
was full of foreigners : Charlotte discovered this
immediately, and was and continued to be
horrified at the outward signs of the Catholic
religion and Catholics' ways of life. Shyness,
added to intolerance, isolated her and her sister :
the two can be pictured, avoiding their fellow-
pupils and walking up and down the avenue of
the Pensionnat garden, a lonely, linked couple in
old-fashioned clothes. Emily persisted in wear-
ing out-of-date leg of mutton sleeves and lank
skirts, and was, of course, completely unsociable,
silent even with English friends of the Taylors at
school near by, who often invited the Brontë girls
to spend the weekly *jour de vacance* at their house.
Charlotte might have donned a frill or flounce
occasionally if Emily had not been there to snort
at any departure from the Parsonage style of dress
– it was more timidity than scorn of new fashions
which kept Charlotte a guy – and if Lucy Snowe's
conversations with Ginevra Fanshawe were like
Charlotte's own with an English fellow-pupil, she
was at least open to conversation, though on her
side, generally, of a reproving and snubbing kind.
Still, evidently, Lucy could not altogether resist
Ginevra's chatter about her young men and had
a soft corner in her embittered heart for that
flighty young lady.

Yet it is because Charlotte was so narrow-
minded, " superior " and solitary that *Villette* is
a great book. A genial, open-hearted and open-
minded person could not have written it, would
not have gone through, really or imaginatively,

the tremendous experience of which that story tells. The experience is the advent of love (the word advent suits Charlotte's religious view of this emotion), much longed for but almost despaired of, into an emotionally starved life. Only a pent-up soul, such as Charlotte's was, under the lock and key of principles as strong as the ardent nature they imprisoned, could have poured that one, sincere, lofty, all-pervasive spirit into the facts, on the face of them as dull as ditch-water, of a priggish, unlovable and unloving governess's career in a foreign town. The artless, straightforward course of the narrative, the clear-cut distinctness of the sketches and portraits, the prompt, unhesitating judgments contained in them, not unjust, certainly, but lacking in kindliness,[1] show the almost wilful aloofness of the narrator from the world she is confronting, reveal, too, the real, though unacknowledged, *raison d'être* of her being there, namely an intense, hungry quest for personal happiness which, consciously, of course, she has dismissed as a vain hope. Charlotte's observation is remarkable, but it is an observation nearly always of deficiencies from her own very narrow, rigidly held standards of conduct, dictated by personal soreness and the behaviour she had subconsciously assumed to cover that soreness up. She cannot even look at a

[1] Charlotte was extremely suspicious of kindly feelings in herself. The reader of *Villette* comes across the following sentence with surprise and amusement. Lucy is talking of Paulina and says: "I liked her. It is not a declaration I have often made concerning my acquaintance in the course of this book; the reader will bear with it for once." The reader is indeed happy to bear with it.

picture – witness her remarks upon the " Cleopatra " in the gallery – without treating the subject of it as a sort of photographic rival of all well-
brought-up, modest and hard-working women
like herself. " She was, indeed, extremely well
fed : very much butcher's meat . . . must she
have consumed to attain that breadth and height,
that wealth of muscle, that affluence of flesh. She
lay half-reclined on a couch – why, it would be
difficult to say ; broad daylight blazed round her.
She appeared in hearty health, strong enough to
do the work of two plain cooks . . . she had no
business to lounge away the noon on a sofa. She
ought likewise to have worn decent garments – a
gown covering her properly, which was not the
case. Out of abundance of material – seven and
twenty yards, I should say, of drapery " (one can
see Charlotte checking it) " -she managed to make
inefficient raiment. Then for the wretched un-
tidiness surrounding her there could be no excuse.
Pots and pans – perhaps I ought to say vases and
goblets – were rolled here and there on the foreground ; a perfect rubbish of flowers was mixed
among them and an absurd and disorderly mass
of curtain upholstery smothered the couch and
cumbered the floor."

To Charlotte, whose tired eyes, on waking in
the morning, fell on the night lamp dying on the
black circular stand in the middle of the dormi-
tory and who had to take gulps of ice-cold water
from her *carafe* to quench her chagrin before she
could settle down to the daily round, this Sybaritic
display was quite unbearable. Insult, too, was

added to injury, for the picture was " set up in the best light, having a cordon of protection stretched before it " and a cushioned bench in front for the accommodation of worshippers. Lucy, be it observed, sat on this bench, so absorbed in her annoyance with Cleopatra's improprieties as not to notice M. Emanuel's approach from behind.

Yet, with all the rancour of which the above is a specimen, goes – and those who study human nature will not need to have the connection explained – a continuity of sincere and exalted feeling of the spiritual dignity of the narrator and the almost cosmic importance of her fate which gives the story an epic grandeur and even turns the snubs which Lucy so often administers to trifling mortals into impressive rebukes. Rhetorical the book is to modern readers ; absurdly over-serious to modern, light-hearted habits of thought ; over-strained in its idealism of love and all the stages of approach to it ; but these sententious dialogues with Reason, these neophytic invocations of the Deities of Hope and Happiness, are the solemnities of intense feeling and conscience, the pomp and state of excessive (pathetically excessive and over-sensitive) self-respect. Lucy Snowe, the unhappy, love-starved, morbidly self-conscious governess, attains, through pain and tribulation, a glorious apotheosis. She has despaired ; she has struggled ; she has schooled herself to hopelessness ; she has rigorously held " the quick of her nature in a catalepsy and a dead trance " ; her struggles have been rewarded ;

M. Emanuel, from his all-seeing window, has pursued them with a determination equal to her resolution ; by her very stoicism she has won for herself an immortal Happiness which, on the last page, the Heavens themselves open to bestow.

Charlotte Brontë, in reality, we know did not reach this Happiness. That she *would have been* in love with M. Héger, if circumstances had allowed, can hardly be denied, in view of the letters she wrote to him, when back again at Haworth after her second visit to Brussels ; but as M. Héger's feelings for her were, obviously, not those of M. Emanuel for Lucy Snowe, and as Charlotte just as evidently was aware of this, it is not fair to say that she *was* in love with him. To one of her disposition, there was all the difference in the world between the earlier stages of romantic feeling and the supreme state of realising "As I love, loved am I" ; not just the difference of Browning's " the little less and what worlds away," for that was expressed in secure retrospect from " the little more and how much it is " and so the poet was able to minimise the last, actual, transforming step. But Charlotte never reached such haven ; the " worlds away " distance remained to her illimitable, untransformed ; only in imagination was her love returned. Had it been otherwise, *Villette* might never have been written ; for happiness does not make for the writing of great love-stories, it is from unhappiness that romance of the *Villette* order is born. And Charlotte, had she been in love with M. Héger,

despite indifference from him or insufficient re-
sponse, would never have made *Villette* hinge on
the miseries of un-cared-for-ness and culminate in
the joy of reciprocated emotion ; her Lucy would
have been a warm-hearted, impetuous, unself-
conscious creature, more alive to the charms of
her fellow-creatures than acutely critical of their
defects. " Being in love," to Charlotte, was a
going out of her whole suppressed nature to someone unmistakably devoted to herself. She says
somewhere in *Villette*, speaking as Lucy, that
she could never resist the impulse to like anyone
who was kind to her – a very natural and touching admission – and the book is dominated by
that attitude. " Being in love " meant a blissful
state of freedom from tormenting comparisons
between her own appearance and pretty, lively,
fascinating girls like Ginevra Fanshawe, agonising
convictions that she, Charlotte, was so plain and
insignificant that no man who looked at her once
would ever willingly look at her again ; it meant
that her intellectual powers would be honoured,
her character valued, her long struggle to put
duty before inclination rewarded ; that dream of
being someone, achieving something, would be
realised, that peace from the terrors of loneliness,
and happiness and joy would come. " Being in
love " without invitation or, at least, without
encouragement, was not in Charlotte's power ;
she distrusted her fellow-creatures, and that
colossal inferiority complex which she called
" Reason " took her to task brutally and jeered
at her whenever the faintest hope glimmered in

her heart. The self-mortification she then under-
went left no " being in love " but a shrunken,
bitter " being in despair." One must remember,
also, that conventional considerations played a
part in shocking Charlotte out of any temptation
to one-sided love. For all her defiance of the
Victorian convention that forbade women to feel
passionately at all, imposing upon them a strictly
passive rôle even with their avowed lovers, she
was conventionally proud, and when, in *Shirley*,
she declared that " no purest angel need blush
to love " she was, of course, assuming the existence of another angel who had already manifested his intentions towards the unblushing
one.

Charlotte and Emily were together for nine
months in Brussels. Miss Branwell was taken ill
suddenly in October 1842, and, as the news was
alarming, they decided to go home at once. Their
aunt was dead before they reached Haworth.
During their absence, Mr. Weightman, also, had
died ; Martha Taylor, too, had died recently, at
the Château de Kockleberg in Brussels, where,
with her sister Mary, she had been a *pensionnaire*.
It was a gloomy homecoming and the hopeful
mood in which Charlotte had left the Parsonage
in February was snuffed out. Nevertheless, she
made up her mind to return to Brussels after
Christmas. The dull sameness of home, probably,
had something to do with that decision, though
M. Héger's letter to Mr. Brontë praising the abilities and characters of his late pupils and deploring
the interruption of their studies which, he said,

needed only a little more time *pour être menés à bonne fin* may have had more to do with it. Emily did not return with Charlotte : no doubt she was glad to be wanted at home, now that " Aunt " was dead and Anne was resuming her situation with the Robinsons where Branwell was also joining her as a tutor. The girls were now possessed of a little money under their aunt's will. That will was made in 1833, a fact which should dispose of Mrs. Gaskell's statement that Branwell was not " remembered " in it because of his " reckless expenditure " ; for Branwell, at the date of the will, was only sixteen, when much was still hoped of him, which was probably the reason why his aunt left him only her " Japan dressing-box " and divided her small savings among her three Brontë nieces and another niece in Cornwall. Charlotte, Emily and Anne bene-fitted to the amount of a little more than three hundred pounds each, as Miss Branwell's estate was proved at the sum of £1500, and these small legacies must have seemed riches to them ; Charlotte, later, told Mrs. Gaskell that she would have been thankful to have had as much pocket money as a penny a week at the age of eighteen.

So a second journey to Brussels came within Charlotte's own means, after her aunt's death, especially as it was now arranged that she was to return as a teacher and to receive a salary of £16 a year. She wanted to improve her knowledge of German, the better to be able, later on, to start a school of her own, and admiration for M. Héger

would not have caused her to return if this object
had not been a genuine one. She had little regard
for anyone else in the Pensionnat ; she felt exceedingly solitary in Brussels. The foreign ways jarred,
and M. Héger, to whom she had not yet begun
to give English lessons, probably only appeared
as a redeeming feature of an otherwise, in many
ways, uncongenial life. Her letters home and to
Ellen show this and show too the ups and downs
of her relationship with the " black swan," as she
called M. Héger. He was evidently critical of her
general unamiability and was, or appeared to her
to be, spasmodic in his kindness to her, loading
her with books to read from time to time, but
anxious, naturally, not to incur gossip or his wife's
jealousy by being the only person to whom Charlotte cared to talk. Charlotte, no doubt, interested
him – " foreigners " are, as a rule, very ready to
be interested in English people – she was serious,
intelligent and ambitious and her pride attracted
as well as provoked the impetuous, tempera-
mental, demonstrative little man. As time passed,
and Charlotte became more and more oppressed
by her loneliness – especially in the summer when
her English friends had left the town – the fitful-
ness of M. Héger's apparent interest in her must
have become something on which she brooded,
often misconstruing the cause and, it goes without saying, for one circumstanced as she was, setting such store on the occasional *tête-à-tête* that
an intense emotional stress was engendered and
many of the symptoms associated with being in
love were set up. Matters came to a crisis in the

autumn of 1843, after a wretched August and
September during which time, the whole household being away on their holidays, Charlotte,
more forlorn than ever, wandered about Brussels
" trying to get a clearer acquaintance with the
streets," and once was so overcome by her loneliness that she, an ultra Protestant, sought the con-
solation of outpouring in a confessional in Ste.
Gudule. The school re-assembled ; the Belgian
hubbub in which Charlotte took no interest – indeed, it desolated her – started again. Unable to
bear it any longer, Charlotte gave Mme. Héger
notice to leave. M. Héger would not hear of it ;
there was evidently a scene out of which Charlotte drew enough comfort to stay on. But by
Christmas, her misery had festered again : M.
Héger probably had not been able to manifest
continuously the warm, if not heated, concern of
his manner during the October interview. Charlotte packed up her boxes and left on New
Year's Day. " I suffered much before I left
Brussels," she wrote to Ellen. " I think, however
long I live I shall not forget what the parting with
M. Héger cost me ; it grieved me so much to
grieve him who has been so true and disinterested
a friend. . . ." " There are times now," she continued, " when it appears to me as if all my ideas
and feelings, except a few friendships and affections, are changed from what they used to be :
something in me, which used to be enthusiasm,
is tamed down and broken. I have fewer illusions ; what I wish for now is active exertion – a
stake in life."

GB

But the truth was that Charlotte's zeal for education had not been as strong as her bitterly suppressed longing for personal happiness.

She reached home, where the problem of the future awaited her. Everyone asked what she was going to do next. She did not know. She had no energy. She was miserable alone with Emily and her father, whose blindness was getting worse. Branwell and Anne continued in their situations with the Robinsons. More curates came and went. Charlotte had her usual fling at them in letters to Ellen, dangling a Mr. Smith, as she had dangled Mr. Weightman, before Ellen's eyes and highly contemptuous of the narrow-mindedness of her future husband, Mr. Nicholls. She returned to the idea of opening a school at the Parsonage. Cards of terms, offering board and education to " a limited number of Young Ladies " at a charge of £35 a year, were printed and sent out. The " limited number " were to be housed in an additional room which Aunt's legacy would enable to be built. The cards fell upon stony ground : no pupils were obtainable. As Emily wrote in the memorandum written on her birthday, July 30th, 1845, intended to be opened three years later, " the school scheme . . . was found no go." " Now I don't desire a school at all," continued Emily, " and none of us have any great longing for it. We have cash enough for our present wants, with a prospect of accumulation. We are all in decent health, only that Papa has a complaint in his eyes, and with the exception of B. who, I hope, will be better and do better hereafter. I am quite contented for myself : not as idle as formerly, altogether as hearty and having learnt to make the most of the present and long for the future with less fidgetiness that I cannot do all I wish ; seldom or ever troubled with nothing to do, and merely desiring that everybody could be as comfortable as myself and as undesponding, and then we should have a very tolerable world of it."

The earlier part of the note, after the characteristic chronological opening, is about a two days' expedition Anne and Emily had made together to York, a month previously, during which excursion they were " Ronald Macalgin, Henry Angora, Juliet Augusteena, Rosabella Esmaldan, Ella and Julian Egremont, Catherine Navarre and Cordelia Fitzaphnold, escaping from the palaces of instruction to join the Royalists who are hard driven, at present, by the victorious Republicans." " The Gondals still flourish bright as ever," wrote Emily. " I am at present writing a work on the First War." But, according to Anne's memorandum of the same date, she was also writing some poetry and it was in the autumn of this year, 1845, Charlotte tells us, that she " accidentally lighted " on a manuscript volume of verse in Emily's handwriting. Miss Romer Wilson has taken Charlotte severely to task for this discovery and accuses her almost of treachery for reading the poems and getting Emily to agree to publication. Such an accusation seems unjustifiable. Emily had an iron will and could not be coerced. She may have been furious with

Charlotte when the latter told her she had read the poems – " it took hours," Charlotte says, " to reconcile her to the discovery I had made " – but this is often the case with intensely reserved and sensitive people when discovery of secrets is made within that half curious, half indifferent circle " the family " whose curiosity is so quiescent at times, so alive at others, that strategy is apt to become careless.   Nevertheless, when the discovery was made and Emily, on her side, discovered that her elder sister's interest was not patronising, but genuine admiration, though it may have taken days to persuade her to publish and face public criticism, she was probably not averse to being persuaded.   " Water will wear away a stone," says Miss Romer Wilson, intimating that Charlotte nagged at Emily until she won. But Charlotte, who could not get Emily to go to bed when she was dying and who tells us that to the influence of other minds Emily was never amenable, would have known that nagging was useless. Besides, Anne, who adored Emily, would not have produced her own poems for inspection had she thought that Emily was being coerced. It was probably much more a matter of overcoming Emily's diffidence, set into pride, than her resentment, and Anne may have brought out her poems as much to help in this as to win praise, too, from Charlotte.

Moreover, the fact that Charlotte herself was diffident ought to dispose of the " nagging " suggestion. It was not as if she had been bent on publishing and, consequently, on getting her sisters to co-operate. Though all of them, Charlotte tells us, had very early cherished dreams of one day becoming authors, these were only vague dreams, at any rate, in Charlotte's mind, otherwise she would not have been engrossed in the plan of a school for so long, in fact, until the failure of their poor little advertisement. Emily had the most definite literary ambitions of the three, if one can judge from the part-picture of her in " Frances " in *The Professor*. But " to become an author " in those days was a profoundly serious undertaking and would-be authors approached publishers and that great Personage, the Public, with awe and reverence. Charlotte's account of how she and her sisters came to take the plunge into print is steeped in nervous dread. To have nagged at Emily to get her to agree to what she herself had hardly yet ventured to contemplate as a practical step could not have occurred to her.

The poems of Currer, Ellis and Acton Bell were published in one small volume by Aylott & Jones of Paternoster Row in the early summer of 1846. " All . . . that merits to be known are the poems of Ellis Bell," wrote Charlotte four years later, and she was right. The little volume, which cost it authors nearly £50 to publish and advertise, and of which, in the year following publication, only two copies were sold, contained twenty-one poems by Emily, among them some of her best and nearly all showing the beautiful directness and intensity of her poetic instinct. She is a supreme poet to those who love undecorated expression of emotion.

It must be pointed out that though Emily's poems are her most personal revelation they are rarely open to the autobiographical interpretation which some biographers have insisted on giving them. One such interpretation, for instance, which assumes that Emily had a lover who died in early youth, is based on the fine poem " Remembrance," which begins :

"Cold in the earth and the deep snow piled above thee."

This poem, as is shown by the heading of one of the two manuscripts of it, was originally written for the Gondal saga and is the lament of Rosina for her murdered husband, King Julius of Angora. It is in the Gondal poems which, like Charlotte's Angrian poems, may have been originally incorporated in prose tales, that Emily voices the depth and intensity of her absorption in those imaginary heroes with whose adventures she and Anne were so often occupied. The Gondal tales are lost ; Anne's notes on the geography of Gondal-land alone remaining, and it needs great interest and patience on the part of the reader of the poems to disentangle from them the outlines of the fortunes of King Julius who, for love of proud, ambitious Rosina, usurped the throne in violation of his oath and met his death at the hands of an avenger, and the fate of his daughter, Augusta, who succeeded him. The mixture of the elemental passions of love, hate and revenge which dominates the poems, and *Wuthering Heights* as well, no doubt, drew from some unresolved conflict in Emily's breast, the emotional tension and tone of which she was acutely familiar with, but psychical processes are strangely devious and illogical, and the rationalised expression of a complex is far from being a replica, or a direct inversion, of the original drama.

The sisters' venture into publication was known to no one but themselves. Branwell, at this time, was in no condition to be joined in the secret. While tutor to the Robinsons, where he was with Anne, from the beginning of 1843, he had developed a violent passion for Mrs. Robinson which, though she was seventeen years older than he was, he fancied was reciprocated. His delusions were so fixed that his family evidently were deceived by his story, as is shown by Mrs. Gaskell's repetition of it, drawn from Charlotte, in the first edition of her book. It is not known whether Branwell had taken to opium before he went to the Robinsons – De Quincey's *Confessions* were published in Branwell's boyhood – but upon his dismissal from Thorp Green, which occurred in the summer of 1845, he certainly had recourse to it and to whisky. Letters from him to his friends reveal a pitiable condition of collapse from which he never recovered. He became a monomaniac on this subject and when, about a year later, Mr. Robinson died, leaving his widow well provided for under her marriage settlement and benefitting under his will to the extent of a life interest in his estate during widowhood, Branwell proceeded to the invention of a crowning calamity and circulated the story that Mrs. Robinson would have married him had she not been prohibited from doing so by the terms of her husband's will. On this last myth, Charlotte admits in a letter to Ellen: "I do not know how much to believe of what he says, but I fear she" (i.e. Mrs. Robinson, said by Branwell to have become insane from misery) "is very ill." "Branwell declares that he neither can nor will do anything for himself; good situations have been offered him more than once, for which, by a fortnight's work, he might have qualified himself, but he will do nothing except drink and make us all wretched." Charlotte, who had tackled her own not dissimilar trouble with fortitude, had no sympathy whatever for her weak brother. Emily had more, as the fine poem "The Wanderer from the Fold," evidently written on her brother's death, shows, the last lines of which –

> *But yet my heart will be*
> *A mourner still, though friend and lover*
> *Have both forgotten thee –*

suggest that she believed Branwell's account of Mrs. Robinson's love for him. But Emily's sympathy was more pitiful than invigorating and Branwell's own vanity and self-pity stood insuperably in the way of his recovery. Brought up, petted, as he had been, the disgrace which his family felt at his conduct and which Charlotte, especially, could not help showing, had a disastrous effect; physically and morally weak, he could not conquer his

> *Sense of past youth and manhood come in vain*
> *Of genius given, and knowledge won in vain.*

He sank into being, not the wildly dissipated maniac that some writers have portrayed, and that Charlotte's sweeping references or avoidance of the subject of him suggest, but that sorriest of figures, a pathetic failure, prematurely old, chronically bronchitical, drinking at times, but not continuously, yet still maintaining for some of his friends the old fascination of talk, the old charm of manner that seemed to them to give the lie to the lurid stories of him that were afterwards spread. He read, and wrote, spasmodically, dreary verses ; he was constantly in the village, and according to one account, basked occasionally in the sunshine of being known to be a brother of the author of *Jane Eyre*. Charlotte's statement that Branwell was never aware that his sisters had published a line cannot, in view of other evidence, be accepted. She may have meant by it that she, personally, had never discussed her books with him, but even this is open to doubt. That Branwell wrote *Wuthering Heights*, or even had a hand in writing it, seems quite untenable. Apart from all external evidence, it is clear from the spirit, style and construction, both of the novel and the poems, that Emily wrote the book.

CHAPTER VII

THE novels – Charlotte's *The Professor*, Emily's *Wuthering Heights* and Anne's *Agnes Grey* – were evidently under way in the winter of 1845–6. In April 1846, Charlotte wrote to the publishers of the poems telling them that " C. E. & A. Bell " were then " preparing for the press " a work of fiction consisting of three distinct and unconnected tales which could be published either together or separately, and enquiring whether they, Aylott & Jones, would consider publication. Aylott & Jones were not prepared to publish fiction and so the novels went on a round to various publishers, at first together, afterwards separately ; at least, Charlotte's MS. separately from the MSS. of her sisters. They were not soon accepted ; their authors grew accustomed to the sight of returned parcels but, undauntedly, sent them forth again. Eventually, *Wuthering Heights* and *Agnes Grey* were accepted – " on terms somewhat impoverishing to the two authors," so Charlotte, unaccustomed to publishers' terms, naïvely wrote – by Mr. Newby of Mortimer Street, who published the two tales together in December 1847. *The Professor* was less fortunate but it acted, nevertheless, as a herald of *Jane Eyre* for, in returning it as too short,

Smith & Elder wrote so civil a letter that Charlotte was consoled and almost immediately sent them *Jane Eyre*, the work in three volumes which they had offered to read.

Jane Eyre was accepted and was published in October 1847. It was a success from the first. " Decidedly the best novel of the season," said *The Westminster Review*, and other reviews followed suit. (The famous *Quarterly Review* attack did not come until a year later.) *Jane Eyre* took London by storm ; people declared that they had sat up all night reading it, a remark which was not then so much a part of reviewers' stock-in-trade as it is now, and Currer Bell suddenly became the most talked-of writer in literary circles everywhere.

Charlotte Brontë, in her quiet way, was immensely excited. She wrote constantly, if not, at first, incessantly, to Smith & Elder's reader, Mr. W. S. Williams. She wrote, of course, always as " yours respectfully, C. Bell,"[1] but the handwriting, apart from the dignified volubility of the letters, can hardly have left Mr. Williams long in doubt as to the sex of Currer Bell. Charlotte, indeed, was in her element in this correspondence, discussing not only her review notices with Mr. Williams, who sent them to her, but also her reviewers and readers (among them Mr. Thackeray and Mr. Lewes) ; enquiring as to the personality

[1] Charlotte had conducted the correspondence with Aylott & Jones under her own name, though always referring to the Bells as the authors but identifying herself with them by using the pronouns " we " and " us. " She had also revealed her sex to Aylott & Jones by directing the proofs of the poems to be sent to " Miss Brontë, *not* C. Brontë, Esq."

and standing of these grandees, enjoying surmises as to the identity of the brothers Bell, telling Mr. Williams about the "delays and procrastinations" Ellis and Acton Bell were enduring at the hands of Mr. Newby, speaking also of Ellis and Acton themselves. "*Wuthering Heights* is, I suppose, at length published, at least Mr. Newby has sent the authors their six copies," she writes on December 14th, 1847. "I wonder how it will be received. I should say it merits the epithets of 'vigorous' and 'original' much more decidedly than *Jane Eyre* did. *Agnes Grey* should please such critics as Mr. Lewes, for it is 'true' and 'unexaggerated' enough. The books are not well got up – they abound in errors of the press. On a former occasion I expressed myself with perhaps too little reserve regarding Mr. Newby, yet I cannot but feel, and feel painfully, that Ellis and Acton have not had the justice at their hands that I have had at those of Messrs. Smith & Elder."

Printers' errors were not Ellis' and Acton's only grievance against their publisher. Mr. Newby, during the summer of 1848, had a brain wave with regard to advertisement which upset the Bells terribly. A reviewer, trying to be clever, had remarked that *Wuthering Heights* was evidently an earlier attempt of the pen which had produced *Jane Eyre*. Mr. Newby, who was then seeking to dispose of Anne's second book, *The Tenant of Wildfell Hall*, in America, saw the value of that remark for advertisement purposes, in view of *Jane Eyre's* success, and expressed his opinion to an American publisher that all the novels were the work of one writer. It is unlikely that this caused any prejudice against *Wuthering Heights*. Charlotte's supposition that it did, which she dwells on with such strong feeling in the biographical sketch of her sisters, was based, apparently, on nothing more substantial than the fear that reviewers and the public would "look darkly" upon what they believed to be a cheat. But, as obviously no cheat had been perpetrated, seeing that the author of *Wuthering Heights*, by calling herself "Ellis Bell," quite clearly had not attempted "to palm off an inferior and immature production under cover of the success of *Jane Eyre*" (though had a cheat been intended, such a course would have been perfectly possible), it is difficult to see how Charlotte arrived at this conclusion and it may, therefore, be assumed that she was here merely casting about for any reason which might explain why Emily's book was not an immediate success. Yet her own attitude to *Wuthering Heights*, as revealed in the well known Preface to its second edition, shows well enough why it was not popular. Indeed, Charlotte's unconcealed horror of her sister's creation still haunts the minds of readers and few critics have not been overpowered by her fine sentences into an adoption of her emotional reactions to the book. But, in fact, such reactions are abnormal and, splendid as Charlotte's Preface is as a piece of writing, and moving as were the circumstances in which it was written, it cannot be regarded as an understanding criticism ; it is a great pity that the Preface is nearly always printed with the book. *Wuthering*

Heights is a " Primitive " in literary art. Its power strikes from its very primitiveness, both of form and expression. Romanticism, the romanticism of Hoffmann, for instance, of his story, *Die Majorat* (*The Entail*), quite possibly influenced Emily Brontë's choice of plot. But there the romantic influence stops and stark realism begins. The German romantics and their followers were not realists ; they were theatrical through and through, in their dialogue, their emotions and their morals. Emily's north country realism, for all that it was concerned with a " stagey " plot, introduced a note which was completely foreign to the taste of fiction readers of that time, a note of primitive passion which not even Charlotte understood.

The story begins as if it were a diary written by a Mr. Lockwood, a stranger to the north country, who announces that his object in renting Thrushcross Grange, from which he writes, is to find solitude. Immediately, however, or so it appears, upon his arrival, Lockwood had rushed off to pay a call on his landlord, Mr. Heathcliff – " the solitary neighbour that I shall be troubled with " – who lived four miles away at a lonely farm house, Wuthering Heights. " A perfect misanthropist's Heaven," and Heathcliff " a capital fellow," writes Lockwood, on his return from the visit which, as he describes it, cannot have been agreeable. Heathcliff received him suspiciously and no sooner did Lockwood enter the house than a pack of rough dogs attacked him savagely. " An absolute tempest of yelping and worrying " ensued, only put an end to by the cook rushing in with her frying pan to belabour the animals, and Heathcliff, though offering wine and relaxing into conversation, showed no sign of wanting to see his visitor again. But the very next day, the lover of solitude repeats his visit, quite insensitive to the fact that he is not wanted, impertinently curious as to the relationship existing between the people he finds there – Heathcliff, a beautiful, fierce young woman and a boorish young man – childishly aggrieved because he does not get a warm reception and morbidly petulant because, when a snow-storm descends, no one takes the least interest in his anxiety to get home. He is allowed to spend the night there and spends it in a cheerlessness which develops into horror, for, by a nightmare and the panic-stricken appearance at his bedside of Heathcliff who has heard his shriek, there is revealed to him the ghost of a passion which has haunted Heathcliff for twenty years. The next day, exhausted by cold and shock, Lockwood returns to the Grange and falls ill. During his illness, Mrs. Dean, the housekeeper, beguiles his weary hours by the full story of that terrible passion. Lockwood recovers, and leaves the neighbourhood but returns a year later to hear the most recent chapter of happenings and himself to be a spectator of the last chapter of all. But the reader, from first to last, is not interested in Lockwood. He does not gain our sympathy by the way in which he forces himself upon the Wuthering Heights household nor do we feel interested in his attempt to make himself seem interesting and to indicate that, if occasion offered, he might fall a victim to Catherine Heathcliff's charms. This suggestion is introduced several times in the book, appearing most wishy-washy by contrast with the tale of terrific passion which Mrs. Dean unfolds. It may be that Emily Brontë at first contemplated making Lockwood's adventures an important part of the story but found that this would not work and so let Lockwood fade out and did not trouble to remove the scaffolding of the original plan.

It is the background, the Past, which lives. The foreground, the Present, never lives ; it is overwhelmed by the Past, though the reminders of the Present, the realisation, from time to time, that Mrs. Dean is telling Lockwood the events of past years leading up to the present day (the year 1801) do, probably, give extra substantiality to those past events, the wreckage of which is *there* at Wuthering Heights, up on the moors, four miles away from *here*, Thrushcross Grange, to be seen as Lockwood himself has just seen it a few days before. Mrs. Dean herself was an important eye-witness of those past events, indeed much more than an eye-witness, an actor in them, closely acquainted with the other actors as only a servant of the old type who lived and grew up with her master's family could be.

It may be for this reason, for the sake of heightening the reader's sense of reality, that writers, particularly early novel writers, have so often adopted the device of writing a story as if it were being narrated by someone who had taken part in what the story tells. It is a primitive device and, like all primitive technique, it is effective partly because its very defects appear not as defects but as perfectly natural limitations. Its advantages are obvious. It permits of a much greater freedom in presenting the facts than when they are set down in the third person by the author. The author is presumed by the reader to know everything there is to know about his characters. The fictional narrator is not expected to know everything ; it would seem unnatural if he seemed to know all. He cannot know all : he was not there at every point in the story. As a real person, he could not have been there. Consequently, there is nothing odd in his being unable to explain certain things. He can get over any difficulty by saying : " What happened, I don't know, but the next thing I knew was . . ." and he can thus pass swiftly and with cogency, even though all sorts of links are left out, from one dramatic situation to another. He can ramble ; he can digress ; he can be quite informal ; and his tale will be none the worse for being unevenly told. Its unevenness and informality will suggest the stamp of truth.

The disadvantages of this way of writing are, of course, that it *cannot* explain everything. Its ability to go into details and to make certain connections is limited by the physical and mental powers of the fictional narrator who cannot pretend to know all that passed behind the scenes, unless he is prepared to acknowledge himself as an eavesdropper, which will spoil the reader's

Hʙ

confidence in him. And, even if he eavesdrops,
he cannot penetrate into his characters' minds,
and so his account must be confined to the more or
less superficial aspects of what happened. But
these drawbacks are not looked upon as drawbacks by the amateur writer who may not be
quite sure how to tackle the behind-the-scenes
part of the business. He sees in the method a way
of avoiding difficulties which he is not yet expert
enough to overcome, and further, not being any
less excited by his subject than the experienced
writer, indeed being probably more excited than
an old hand just because he does not know exactly
how he is going to convey what he very intensely
feels, he seizes on one sure way of convincing his
readers of the reality of his story. He provides a
narrator who saw, as it were, the story with his
own eyes and whose direct evidence will be
conclusive.

> *Who saw him die ?*
> " *I*," *said the fly*,
> " *With my little eye.*
> *I saw him die.*"

" I saw him die." That is enough. The scene
immediately becomes vivid. Once reality is
established by direct evidence, the imaginations
of readers get to work. Cock Robin's death scene
lives and how many words are saved !

Emily Brontë was not content with one fictional
narrator. She took it into her head to try to
double-stage her scenario, to build a foreground
for the narrator to live in, as substantial as the

background behind. She did not succeed, perhaps fortunately. For, if the tiresome Lockwood had forced his own affairs, possibly a love affair with the youthful Catherine, upon the reader's attention, not only would that have interfered with our view of the central tragedy but it would have marred the extraordinary symmetry of the interwoven fates of the two families of Earnshaw and Linton, and of the web spun by Heathcliff's passionate revenge.

Nevertheless, this trick of double-staging effects changes in the reader's perspective from time to time which do undoubtedly tell. They tell in the sense that they mitigate the violence of the story, subdue a feeling of horror in the mind of the reader, by recalling to him again and again the fact that that which at the moment is rousing his horror is over now, happened years ago, has receded into the Past. Emily Brontë uses Time, much as Thomas Hardy uses it, to temper the spectacle of human passion, to impart to the reader a tenderness almost towards those who in life went so far astray. We do not only think of that passage at the close of the book where Lockwood, standing in the little moorland churchyard, by the tombstones of the three victims, wondered " how anyone could ever imagine unquiet slumbers for the sleepers in that quiet earth," but of several places in the book where Mrs. Dean's story, told to enliven Lockwood's convalescence, is suddenly broken off, tiresomely, because we kick at the interruption and are not interested in the stages of Lockwood's illness and Mrs. Dean's solicitude lest her patient should be tired by too long gossip, but none the less having the effect of pushing the tragic scene away from us, back into the Past where it belongs, needing no one's tears any more. For visible proof of this, there is Mrs. Dean who has lived through it all, perfectly composed, the " dree story " driven from her mind by a glance at the clock which points to the hour for Lockwood's medicine or gruel.

Mrs. Dean herself is another source of mitigation. Not that her attitude towards what has happened is a tender one : far from it. She is in some ways a crude medium, one through whose eyes subtly perceptive people would be loth to follow, unreservedly, any course of events. She was a respectable, old-fashioned north-country woman, of the type that the Brontës knew so well in the person of their devoted old servant Tabby, going into service in young girlhood, becoming part and parcel of the family she worked for, honest, faithful, outspoken, independent but with a narrow outlook, naturally, and no sensitive understanding of character though shrewd to seize outstanding traits. Born and bred where life is rough and folk, more often than not, are violent in speech and deed, such people are not deeply affected by violence ; they accept it as part of life and meet it unsurprisedly, or at least without lasting perturbation. They do not put themselves about to fathom the causes of strange or wild behaviour, for which very reason their accounts of it are more definite and dramatic than the versions of those who seek an explanation of what is happening, the while they observe. Their speech is rough and ready, graphic with the instant impression, immensely telling because of the way in which, in phrases like that which Mrs. Dean used to describe Heathcliff – " hard as a whin-stone " – it sculptures, in high relief, that instant impression upon the listener's imagination, but not psychologically enlightening. But the vivid picture is what matters to most people ; undoubtedly it mattered a great deal to Emily Brontë. It would be misleading to say that she had a taste for the violent, because that would suggest that she consciously sought it out. She did not consciously seek it. Charlotte was right when she told Mrs. Gaskell that Emily never realised that her story was a shocking one. Life presented itself violently and dramatically to her, first because she had little contact with other than village and moorland people, and that mainly at second-hand through her father's, Tabby's and village talk and tales, and also because she was not a prober into the inner side of happenings, the psychological side – few people were in those days and her own unconquerable shyness and reticence stood in the way. Perhaps, too, we should not be far wrong in thinking that just because she was so shy, she saw life in unusually bare, dramatic lines. For behind that excessive shyness of hers there was probably an unconscious longing, only a little less strong than the shyness, for deeper knowledge of and closer contact with people and things. Cut off from the inner aspect, her concentration upon the outside view of events became the more intense, and so unconsciously she went further in dramatic emphasis than she realised. The material on which her mind worked was dramatic enough, to begin with. In a letter from Mrs. Gaskell on the subject of her stay with Charlotte Brontë at Haworth, published in Miss Haldane's recent book, *Mrs. Gaskell and Her Friends*, Mrs. Gaskell writes :

" On the moors we met no one. Here and there in the gloom of the distant hollows she [Charlotte] pointed out a dark grey dwelling, with Scotch firs growing near them often, and told me such wild tales of the ungovernable families who lived or had lived therein that *Wuthering Heights* even seemed tame comparatively. Such dare-devil people, men especially and women so strong and cruel in some of their feelings, and so passionately fond in others . . . small landed proprietors, dwelling on one spot since Queen Elizabeth. . . . These people build grand houses and live in the kitchens."

And Charlotte herself writes, in the Preface to Emily's book :

" My sister's disposition was not naturally gregarious ; circumstances favoured and fostered her tendency to seclusion : except to go to church or take a walk on the hills she rarely crossed the threshold of home. Though her feeling for the people round was benevolent, intercourse with them she never sought ; nor with very few exceptions, ever experienced. And yet she knew them ; knew their ways, their language, their family histories ; she could hear of them with interest and talk of them with detail, minute, graphic, and accurate : but *with* them she rarely exchanged a word. Hence it ensued that what her mind had gathered of the real concerning them, was too exclusively confined to those tragic and terrible traits of which, in listening to the secret annals of every rude vicinage, the memory is sometimes compelled to receive the impress." And Emily, she goes on to say, could not understand what was meant " if the auditor of her work, when read in manuscript, shuddered under the grinding influence of natures so relentless and implacable." To Emily, Heathcliff was ruthless, cruel in his ruthlessness, violent in his passion for Catherine and his hatred of Earnshaw and Edgar, hard as a whin-stone, but he was not monstrous. He was as so many moorland people were, as Charlotte told Mrs. Gaskell they were. Emily did not shrink from hearing about them or writing about them. She could not tone down their violent behaviour by psychological explanation ; she was too used to hearing of such behaviour to indulge in horrified comments. She was not horrified. Life, as she knew it, was like that. As to passing harsh judgments on such people, leave judgment to God. God who understands will forgive.

Emily had no definite religious views, which fact, as we know, was a source of anxiety to Mrs. Gaskell and others ; but, all the same, she was deeply religious in feeling. She believed in an all-loving, eternal Power who pitied human transgressions and granted rest, in the end, to all sinners. This deep, religiously felt tolerance of

hers which, as her poems show, was as characteristic of her nature as that other characteristic
of violent feeling and manifested itself in *Wuthering
Heights* in the way in which she used Time to
soften the sense of tragedy, took the place in her
mind that a more scientific understanding of the
psychology of human beings takes in the minds of
readers of to-day.   Heathcliff is no more monstrous to us than he was to Emily.   We see him,
at first, as no more than an ill-used sullen boy,
growing bitter under Hindley's ill treatment and
Catherine's apparently uncertain affection and
thoughtless coquetries ; he disappears and we
see him returned and faced with the irrevocable
fact of Catherine's marriage to his loathed rival,
Edgar, and her breakdown and death ; we see
Heathcliff's bitterness and rage hardening into
relentless scheming to wreck the lives and capture
the fortunes of both families, the Earnshaws and
the Lintons ; we see his almost complete triumph,
his haunted pursuit of the mocking spirit of
Catherine and his sudden tormented end.   There
are passages in which Heathcliff is described to
seem literally diabolical, and his mysterious origin
and dark, swarthy appearance – " as black as if
he came from the devil " – as well as the supernatural element in the story are in keeping with
that impression of him, at any rate upon a men-
tality as naturally superstitious as Mrs. Dean's.
And as it is Mrs. Dean who is telling the story
that impression is, of course, conveyed to the
reader.   But, after the book has been read more
than once, reflection suggests that Heathcliff was

not in reality the devil incarnate. Mrs. Dean's inclination at times to see him as such has to be discounted. For one thing, she was, though a superior, still a simple-minded, countrywoman, whose very intellectual shortcomings make for violent impressions and the use of crude similes, and there has also to be taken into account the glimpses of Heathcliff through Lockwood's eyes. Lockwood found Heathcliff surly, inhospitable, ill-natured, but all the same, during his illness, he was thankful to have a visit from him. " I found him very intelligent on the subjects we touched," he reports, unfortunately telling us no more than that.

Lockwood's impression, slight though it is, is clearly more impartial than Mrs. Dean's, and in it we get the only attempt which is made in the book to give an independent view of Heathcliff, perhaps to put into concrete form something of Emily's own wider, though undeveloped, under-standing of the tragedy which finds abstract ex-pression in Lockwood's graveside soliloquy, and is implied in the various shiftings of perspective to which attention has been drawn. The attempt is feebly begun and soon abandoned ; Emily Brontë could not make Lockwood, who did not belong to the moorland world, or his intercourse with the rough characters of that world, real because she had no direct experience of that kind to draw upon. Her experience was of being *told* of moor-land folk and moorland life by the Mrs. Deans of her acquaintance whom she was not afraid to talk to, whose tales, indeed, she relished inordinately, snatching at life as her simple friends saw it rather than, because of her shyness, go without seeing it at all. Hence she could not easily create in writing any form of experience except the one she was familiar with, could not write a story otherwise than as if she had been told it. There is a duality of outlook in the book : the one seemingly akin to Mrs. Dean's, yet in reality not so much akin as dependent on Mrs. Dean's vision ; the other, much more essentially Emily's own, vaguely expressed and unanalysed, would-be understanding and forgiving, yet debarred from clear understanding by lack of experience and so only able to dissociate itself from the crude, black and white judgments of those through whose eyes Emily peered at life by an intensely felt conviction of an understanding, forgiving God. That strong, but unanalysed conviction of hers answers to the more scientific understanding of modern readers who do not find Heathcliff monstrous or diabolical in the literal sense any more than Emily did, only in her case it was religious or charitable feeling which moved her to that conclusion and in modern readers it is a greater knowledge than Emily had of the psychological springs of action and a consequent realisation of how naturally, without any need to bring in a supernatural agency, Heathcliff's cruel behaviour and strange personal obsession can be explained.

In tragic life, God wot,
No villain need be ! Passions spin the plot,
We are betrayed by what is false within.

Heathcliff was no devil, but a passionate, fierce
willed, reckless, undisciplined man, such as wild,
remote places discover and encourage, such as the
moors harboured, as Charlotte told Mrs. Gaskell of
on their walk. Charlotte, certainly, had called
Heathcliff " a man's shape animated by demon
life " in her Preface, but that was because his passion for Catherine outraged her ideal of love.
Charlotte idealised love. She loved the passion
itself. To her, as she wrote in *Shirley*, it was a
" divine virtue," " living fire brought from a
divine altar." She was horrified that it should be
shown as ravaging and reckless, leaving ruin in its
wake. No wonder that she shuddered as she read
and re-read *Wuthering Heights* and questioned
whether it was " right or advisable " to create
beings like Heathcliff ; no wonder that she pro-
tested against acknowledging that love, as she
understood it, had any part in Heathcliff's passion
for Catherine. " A sentiment, fierce and in-
human," she declared that to be, " a passion such
as might boil and glow in the bad essence of some
evil genius ; a fire that might form the tormented
centre, the ever suffering soul of a magnate of the
infernal world." In creating Heathcliff, Emily,
she feared, had been overmastered by her imagination as those who possessed creative gifts were
liable to be.

Emily, herself, would probably have said
" Fudge " to this explanation, not sharing her
sister's illusion as to the divinity of love. For love,
Emily might have said, is a very peculiar thing ;
intense, sacred, if you like to call it so, but when

all is said, atrociously dangerous. Some of its mysteries can be brought to light but still there will remain something in the dark, mysterious, elusive and uncontrollable. Love, she might have said, fiercely, cannot always be domesticated. When we love, there are times when all our wisdom, all our previous consideration of love in the abstract, all our regard for social responsibilities, desert us, and we are helpless. We know in a powerless way that we ought to rule it instead of being ruled by it, but we do not, cannot always succeed.

They would never have agreed, for Charlotte, with all her capacity for passionate feeling and her defiance of the convention that forbade women to show their desire to be loved, had conventional views as regards the nature of love itself. Whereas Emily, unconcerned with conventions, had come more to grips, in imagination, with the real thing. There was a social axiom at issue between Charlotte and women of her generation like Lady Eastlake who, in the *Quarterly Review*, declared the author of *Jane Eyre* to be " a woman who has long forfeited the society of her sex," and Miss Anne Mozley, that good Churchwoman and contributor to the *Christian Remembrancer*. The axiom was that the Victorian lady was devoid of passion and in consenting to marry, was sacrificing her natural maidenly inclinations for the sake of society. There was nothing at issue between Emily and people of such views. Emily's world was one in which society and its conventions had no place. No Lady Eastlake nor Miss Mozley dipped her pen in pious horror to rebuke the author of *Wuthering Heights*. It was received, when it was noticed, as an impersonal creation : the product of a powerful but unpleasant mind. The chief characters were repulsive : the idiom was bare and uncouth : it was rude and strange and violent in a day when a direct display of these qualities was not likely to lead to popular favour or to fame.

Emily was bitterly disappointed at the apparent failure of her novel. The rumour that it was by the author of *Jane Eyre* must have galled her, as also the change of tune in some later reviews as to the respective merits of the authors of the poems. When these were first published, Ellis' poems had been recognised as the best, but when Currer Bell had become famous, her poems were referred to as the outstanding ones. To want success and to be so hopeful of at least a small measure of it that you hide yourself from publicity behind a pseudonym, and then to get scant recognition and further to have your very identity put in doubt is a bitterly disappointing experience. Emily's seeming indifference to and scorn of success were only a mask. Those who doubt her authorship of *Wuthering Heights* should refer to Charlotte's letters to Mr. Williams and to a passage in the before-mentioned letter from Mrs. Gaskell, quoted in Miss Haldane's book, where Mrs. Gaskell says :

" But Emily, poor Emily – the pangs of disappointment as review after review came out about *Wuthering Heights* were terrible. Miss

Brontë said she had no recollection of pleasure or gladness about *Jane Eyre* : every such feeling was lost in seeing Emily's resolute endurance, yet knowing what she felt." And the desolation which encompassed Charlotte when, in 1850, she sat down to write that moving biographical sketch of her sisters was largely the desolation of feeling that the identities of Ellis and Acton Bell had been smothered by the mystery which, she said, she was writing to clear up.

The mystery, however, had existed mainly only in the minds of the Brontë sisters. The public were curious but not mystified, no more curious, however, than they would have been if the three sisters had written under their own names instead of under the neutral ones they chose, so conscientious were they at assuming Christian names not positively masculine. Certainly their own names would have divulged that they were women, but would have conveyed no more than that to the public, who would have said, " Who are the Brontës ? " just as they *did* say, " Who are the Bells ? " The " mystery " had amused Charlotte and her sisters at first but as expectations (which, with budding authors, however modest, are always great) faded and the three names were confused and even the existence of two out of the three doubted, the disguise lost its savour and the inapposite remarks in the reviews which had at first been laughable became galling to read. No wonder that Charlotte, the only one of the three who had scored success and upon whom the mystery had not recoiled, felt, in 1850, that it was time that the obscurity attending the names of Ellis and Acton should be dispelled.

Emily and Anne were dead then. Their long-cherished dream of becoming authors had scarcely been realised, had come to seem almost a farce to them in that miserable autumn after Branwell's death and just before Emily died. On one November afternoon, two years before, the three sisters had sat together over the fire in the very room where Charlotte, in 1850, was writing alone. The *North American Review* had come that day. Charlotte had read bits of it aloud to the other two, thinking that as Emily seemed a little easier, it might amuse her and Anne to hear what a bad lot the Bells were thought to be. As she sat between them, she had studied the two " ferocious authors," as she called them in writing to Mr. Williams that same evening, describing the scene.

" Ellis," she wrote, " ' the man of uncommon talents, but dogged, brutal and morose,' sat leaning back in his easy chair, drawing his impeded breath as he best could and looking, alas, piteously pale and wasted : it is not his wont to laugh, but he smiled, half amused and half in scorn, as he listened. Acton was sewing, no emotion ever stirs him to loquacity, so he only smiled too, dropping at the same time a single word of calm amazement to hear his character so darkly portrayed."

The recollection of this scene, and of many even sadder ones, must have been terribly with her as she sat in the empty silent room, her sisters' books before her, their chairs close by.   *Wuthering*

Heights and *Agnes Grey* were to be republished. If
only Emily and Anne could have known that !
If only she could have seen Emily's half scornful
smile again and Anne's quiet, amazed look !
But they were dead, Emily buried close by in the
church, Anne at Scarborough. Charlotte alone
was left with her old father in the Parsonage, " to
wipe the dust off their gravestones and leave their
dear names free from soil."

Violent grief was over perhaps ; she could not
otherwise have written so calmly. She was writing, not to relieve her feelings of personal loss, nor
to make her sisters known to the public in any
graphic sense. She was writing to protect their
reputations : she had her arms stretched, as it
were, defensively, between them and any im-
pertinent curiosity. " In externals, they were two
unobtrusive women," she wrote, hitting out at
those who had thought them ferocious males. " I
may sum up all by saying," she concluded, rigidly,
" that for strangers they were nothing, for superficial observers less than nothing. . . ." Herein
we have merely the measure of the Victorian
worship of privacy, with its reverse, the horror of
publicity, and no real impression of Emily or
Anne. For strangers, or even superficial observers, Emily, in particular, can never have been
nothing ; her fierce unsociability must have drawn
attention. She was aloof, and never merged, as
unnoticeable people merge, into any company.
There was probably nothing really unobtrusive,
either in appearance or manner, about any of the
Brontës, except perhaps Anne, who was the

gentlest and, though pretty, the most ordinary-looking. Charlotte's smallness was noticeable and Emily's thin figure invariably dressed in lank, unfashionable clothes, and dumb aloofness must have marked her out. But in this biographical notice Charlotte was burying her sisters with solemn honours. In those days, one could not write of the beloved dead in a living way. Impressions had to be subdued into grave sentences ; from the past tense with its absolute finality there was no escape. The gulf between life and death was greater then than it is now. The souls of the dead were with God and for mourners to write naturally about them was not in keeping with the sense of private loss.

So it happened that Emily's personality was shrouded as no doubt Emily herself would have said defiantly that she wished it should be. Charlotte's Preface remained for over thirty years the only biographical account of Emily and it is still, and must always be, the outstanding source of knowledge of her life and character. But it is painfully short and reserved. What would we not have given if Mrs. Gaskell had written down all that Charlotte told her about Emily, of whom, says Mrs. Gaskell, " she was never tired of talking, nor I of listening," or if Charlotte, instead of writing *Shirley*, who was meant to be Emily as she might have been in prosperity, had written a story about Emily as she was in obscurity and unsuccess ! After Emily's death, Charlotte was haunted by recollections of her. She was constantly seeing likenesses to Emily in people whom she met – George Henry Lewes, for example. When she sent a copy of *Shirley* to Mrs. Gaskell, the latter's reply, she said, might have been written by her sister. There are bits of Emily in three of Charlotte's novels ; Diana Rivers in *Jane Eyre*, Frances Evans Henri in *The Professor*, and, of course, Shirley are partly drawn from her. But the poems and *Wuthering Heights*, the very build of which reflects Emily's reticence, as well as the swift, tense style of the writing, utterly different from anything of Charlotte's or Branwell's, are the mirror of Emily's mind.

CHAPTER VIII

The deaths of Branwell, Emily and Anne – Charlotte's marriage
to Mr. Nicholls – her death.

A SECOND edition of *Jane Eyre* came out early in
1848 ; it was dedicated to Thackeray, whom
Charlotte greatly admired. The new edition
prospered, and *Wuthering Heights* (with *Agnes
Grey*) was selling. Anne's second novel, *The
Tenant of Wildfell Hall*, went into a second edition
in this year of its first publication (1848) ; Smith
& Elder had bought the unsold poems from Aylott
& Jones and re-issued them ; so that there were
no grounds for despondency as regards literary
prospects if the three sisters had not afflicted
themselves by brooding on the confusion of their
authorships, to which, of course, review notices,
copying from one another, as reviews do, continued to allude from time to time. But life in the
Parsonage was becoming more and more depress-
ing on account of Branwell, who was by now a
wreck, draining his father and sisters of sleep,
peace of mind and any hopefulness, and keeping
them all in a state of almost rabbit-like apprehension which inquisitiveness from friends as to the
novels seemed to aggravate. They were more
isolated than ever ; Charlotte's letters to Ellen,
who had been told nothing about the writing
but who was suspicious and asked questions, were
perfunctory and deceptive. On one occasion

(May, 1848) she wrote, in answer to an enquiry :
" Whoever has said it – if anyone has, which I
doubt – is no friend of mine. Though twenty
books were ascribed to me, I should own none.
I scout the idea utterly. . . . If then any Birstal-
lian or Gomersallian should presume to bore you
on the subject – to ask you what ' novel ' Miss
Brontë has been ' publishing ' – you can just say,
with the distinct firmness of which you are perfect
mistress, when you choose, that you are authorised
by Miss Brontë to say, that she repels and disowns
every accusation of the kind." Emily and Anne,
following her suit, appear to have been violently
against publicity and when Charlotte told her
father about *Jane Eyre* they would not let their
books be mentioned to him.

The winter of 1847–8, as well as the winter
before that, had been severe : influenza had been
rife, everyone in the Parsonage had been ill with
it, the " animal spirits " of all were much reduced.
Anne was constantly feverish ; the writing of
Wildfell Hall had been a strain on her though not
because, as Charlotte's remarks in the biographical sketch have been understood to indicate,
she had drawn a picture of Branwell therein. The
central figure of *Wildfell Hall* is far from being
like Branwell ; Anne obviously avoided direct
portraiture. The story is of an unhappy marriage,
made in haste and repented of, between an
amiable young woman and a rake who shatters
her fond illusions and himself proceeds along the
primrose path to an untimely but finally contrite
end. Anne, who had seen the beginning of her

brother's infatuation at the Robinsons, when they were together as tutor and governess, could no doubt have written an account of what happened: she was observant, fair-minded and had a quiet humour ; but she was as reticent about this as about everything else. She had been secretly in love with Willie Weightman : he was dead : life for her was very empty and sad : she suffered from religious fears and she was consumptive.

Branwell's health failed fast during this summer but his death on September 24th was unexpected. Charlotte, writing to Mary Taylor in New Zealand at the beginning of September, does not mention Branwell ; her long letter is entirely given up to an account of the visit which she and Anne had made to London, on the spur of the moment, in July, to see their publishers and to dispose, once and for all, of the story that *Wildfell Hall*, recently published, was written, as well as *Wuthering Heights* and *Agnes Grey*, by the author of *Jane Eyre*. Charlotte's impressions, of the interview at Smith & Elder's, of the Opera House where they were taken, of her awful headache in consequence of so much excitement, of the Smiths' house in Bayswater where they dined, were as vivid in September as upon her return to Haworth on July 12th. Branwell was nowhere in her mind then : she had become indifferent to the trouble of his existence. " He is the same as ever " – she writes, rather heartlessly, to Ellen, later on in the same month – " But has not every house its trial ? "

Two months later, Branwell died suddenly.

He was in the village two days before he died and in bed only for one day. His dying state evidently broke the long tension between him and his once favourite sister. A change came over his demeanour and language in the last two days, so Charlotte wrote to Mr. Williams and the Nusseys: " all the bitterness seemed gone," out of herself, too, as well as out of her unfortunate and miserable brother. " All his errors – to speak plainly, all his vices – seemed nothing to me in that moment ; every wrong he had done, every pain he had caused, vanished ; his sufferings only were remembered ; the wrench to the natural affections only was left." Charlotte broke down at Branwell's death, and was in bed for a week with a fever and sick headache. Emily started a cold and cough the following week.

Emily is said to have caught a cold at Branwell's funeral. The cold developed into inflammation of the lungs. She would see no doctor, take no respite from domestic duties. " We saw she was ill, but she never would own it," said Martha, the servant, to Mrs. Gaskell when the latter stayed there, " never would have a doctor near her, never would breakfast in bed – the last morning she got up and she dying all the time, the rattle in her throat while she would dress herself, and neither Miss Brontë nor I dared offer to help her." She died just before Christmas. The last months of her life do not bear thinking of. Charlotte and Anne must have suffered agonies, watching her while she dragged herself about, furious if either of them tried to persuade her to rest. Charlotte's statement of her sister's symptoms, so far as she had been able to find them out, which she wrote for submission, through Mr. Williams, to a London doctor, has a painful fascination. " Her pulse – the only time she allowed it to be felt – was found to be 115 per minute. . . . Her resolution to contend against illness being very fixed, she has never consented to lie in bed for a single day – she sits up from seven in the morning till ten at night. . . . All medical aid she has rejected, insistent that Nature should be left to take her own course."

This was written on December 9th. The London doctor wrote an opinion which Charlotte could not understand and sent some medicine which Emily would not take. She grew daily weaker but more inflexible. They did not realise that she was dying until just before the end. Her fierce independence belied the idea of death. On 19th of December she rose as usual, dressed with terrible difficulty and tottered downstairs to the dining-room. There she collapsed and gasped out that she would see a doctor. But it was too late, and soon after she made an effort to rise from the sofa and fell back – dead.

It was not deliberate suicide. Emily did not want to die. " She was torn, conscious, panting, reluctant, out of a happy life," Charlotte wrote to Ellen later. Emily's awful self-will ; her blind obstinacy ; the family habit of giving in to her, of " not daring " to insist on medical treatment and nursing, were responsible for her death. Poor agonised Charlotte, writhing to avoid facing these responsibilities, found comfort, as was her wont, in an eloquence which was not quite sincere. " I will not now ask why Emily was torn from us in the fullness of our attachment, rooted up in the prime of her own days, in the promise of her powers ; why her existence now lies like a field of green corn trodden down, like a tree in full bearing struck at the root. I will only say, sweet is rest after labour and calm after tempest, and repeat again and again that Emily knows that now."

" She died in a time of promise," she repeated, to Ellen. That was, indeed, true, and to Charlotte, it always remained the great tragedy. She knew, whatever else she did not know about her sister, Emily's outstanding power. She knew that Emily was bigger, far bigger than she herself was. Often, no doubt, there had been friction between the two. Charlotte had an eldest sister side to her which had been too positive, too managing, too inquisitive for Emily's nerves. Charlotte had been unkindly hard on Branwell ; she had embittered herself as well as him by her cold, damning self-righteousness. She had shown no tenderness towards her weak brother : Emily and she may often have been bitterly, though silently, at issue over this. It is, however, impossible to be sure. All we know is that Charlotte, after Emily's death, indeed before her death, during that dreadful time of watching, became aware of the intensity of her love for Emily in a way that seems to show something more than straightforward anguish, a tormenting sense of longing to have understood Emily better. " The two human

beings who understood me, and whom I understood, are gone," Charlotte wrote to Mr. Williams
after Anne died. That was not true, as regards
Emily, but Charlotte need not be blamed for the
lack of understanding. Emily resented attempts
at intimacy. Were she alive to-day, despite all
the attraction that we feel towards her, an attraction partly built up by unsatisfied enquiry and
the legend of her isolation, even with the greater
understanding that we may think that we moderns
possess of natures like hers, we might find ourselves completely daunted. That she made no
close friends shows what excessive fear of self-
betrayal must have dominated her. Had she
lived longer, she might have overcome these
terrors. She was only thirty when she died,
an age which though not young, according to
social standards, is early in the emotional life of
a woman who lived in a remote village and was
handicapped by circumstance and disposition,
as she was, from intercourse with her fellow-
creatures. The tragedy of Emily Brontë's life was
that she died before tasting any of the sweets of
success. She would not have over-rated them ;
she would not have over-valued any of the crucial
joys of life, but that youthful bitterness, that melo-
dramatic despondency of hers would have been
tempered. Her deepest feeling of a universal
harmony, with which the moors inspired her,
would, by degrees, have made trial of, and
accepted or rejected, all the various moods of her
soul which in youth jostle and rub against one
another promiscuously, alternating in control,

mingling sometimes in ugly confusion. At forty, had she lived, she might have smiled indulgently at the unnecessarily Promethean note of " The Old Stoic " :

> *Riches I hold in light esteem,*
> *And Love I laugh to scorn,*
> *And lust of fame was but a dream*
> *That vanished with the morn*

realising then that Life, God, Reality, or whatever other abstraction she was addressing so defiantly in that poem, exists quite regardless of our approval or scorn, our postures, humble or proud, and requires us to be neither its hale champions nor its heroic adversaries.

But she died " in a time of promise," and partly owing to the peculiarities of her disposition and work, partly because of Charlotte's over-shadowing reputation, she remained for years in the background. When, in 1883, Madame Duclaux, then Miss Mary Robinson, was asked to write a life of Charlotte for an Eminent Women series of books, and chose instead to write about Emily, her publishers cut down the fee first offered. Madame Duclaux, a girl herself at that time, had the privilege of visiting Miss Nussey, who lived until 1897, and she saw besides many elderly Haworth villagers who remembered Emily Brontë. But, to quote a saying of Vauvenargues, " *on tire peu des vieillards*," and it is one of life's little ironies that those who happen to have seen " Shelley plain " are rarely those who are best qualified to tell us vital things about him. This

is said without any intention of under-estimating
Miss Nussey's life-long devotion to the memory
of the Brontës, or her generosity in putting her
store of recollections and Charlotte's letters
at the service of so many writers. The story
of those letters and of the vicissitudes of Miss
Nussey's ownership and plans for the disposal of
them deserves a book to itself which might vie in
interest with the tale of intrigue that went on
round Queen Elizabeth in her last days to get her
to declare a successor to her throne. Loyalty to
Charlotte clashed with a natural wish to make a
profitable deal, while fear and cordial dislike of
Mr. Nicholls, " that wicked man who was the
death of dear Charlotte," in whom the copyright
of the letters resided, checkmated her attempts to
publish. She was not an intellectual woman, nor
an imaginative one, but, as Charlotte's friend, she
had often stayed at the Parsonage and was on
affectionate terms with all the sisters and doubt-
less knew Emily as well as anyone outside the
family circle knew that difficult, cranky creature.
No one knew Emily intimately ; not even Anne,
her favourite sister, knew the innermost recesses
of Emily's mind. No record of her, except her
own writings, goes beyond the surface and the
surface impressions do not take us far. There is
Miss Nussey's account of her as a girl of fourteen,
" the tallest person in the house except for her
father . . . with liquid, kindling eyes . . . but she
did not often look at you, she was so reserved."
There are the tributes which Madame Duclaux
drew from villagers, tributes to her kindness,

thoughtfulness and usefulness at home. On the other hand there are impressions left on the minds of some of those who, as school-girls, were at Brussels with her, disagreeable impressions of her abruptness and severity, and there is Sir Clifford Allbutt's boyhood's recollection that "no one could get on with Emily." In Branwell's portrait group, her face is striking but exceedingly difficult to read. It is a proud, scornful face, with an aquiline nose and prominent mouth, set and determined. The eyes are wide apart but there is a look in them abstracted almost to wildness. There is a strong likeness in features but not in expression between Emily and Anne ; between Charlotte and the other two there is little resemblance. Of the three faces, Emily's is the arresting one.

Anne lived five months after Emily's death ; she drooped rapidly from that time. A Leeds doctor whose advice was immediately sought pronounced her lungs to be in an advanced tuberculous condition. Anne was as patient in her illness as Emily had been ruthless. She had but one longing : for the spring to come that she might have a change of air. The spring came but the warmer weather made her worse instead of better. Her wish to go, nevertheless, to Scarborough seemed madness to Charlotte who, accompanied by Ellen Nussey, took her there at Whitsuntide. She was dying when she was carried out of the Parsonage, but it made her happy to see York, where they stayed the night, and the Cathedral, and Scarborough and its bay once more. She went out on the sands in a donkey chair, sat by the lodging-house window (No. 2 Cliff, now pulled down), and looked at the sea which was calm as glass. Then, two days later (May 28th, 1849), she died, conscious to the last and peacefully. She was buried in Scarborough churchyard.

Charlotte stayed on there for a fortnight with Ellen before returning to a desolate home. Yet not quite desolate, Charlotte tried to feel : " Papa is there, and two most affectionate and faithful servants, and two old dogs, in their way as faithful and affectionate – Emily's large house-dog which lay at the side of her dying bed and followed her funeral to the vault, lying in the pew couched at our feet while the burial service was being read – and Anne's little spaniel . . . I am certain they thought that, as I was returned, my sisters were not far behind." . . . " I left papa soon and went into the dining-room. I shut the door. I tried to be glad that I was come home. I have always been glad before – except once ; even then I was cheered. But this time joy was not to be the sensation. . . . The sense of desolation and bitterness took possession of me."

" Labour must be the cure, not sympathy." Pathetic Charlotte, for ever putting herself to school ! With that resolve, she forced her pain-stricken mind to work again ; to finish *Shirley*, already begun ; to edit, in that room haunted by her sisters' presences and memories of evenings spent in writing there and in pacing together round the table, a new edition of *Wuthering Heights* and *Agnes Grey* and another selection of poems ;

to write, through a period of intense depression and physical weakness, her greatest work, *Villette*. She visited London many times ; she met celebrities ; she made new friends. But timidity and self-consciousness of a morbid kind and an old-maidish primness never left her nor did Romance ever come her way. She refused at least another offer of marriage and eventually, in fear and trembling, but determined, engaged herself to her father's curate, Mr. Nicholls. In that marriage, she found, if not a twin soul, at least a husband who was in love with her and whose misery at her first rejection of him had aroused a " Now or never " commotion in her heart. She was settling down into a comfortable, if uninspiring, domesticity at the Parsonage, when she died, in pregnancy, after some weeks of sickness, on March 30th, 1855. There have been few essentially sadder lives than Charlotte Brontë's and perhaps the most pathetic aspect of it lies in the fact that she was probably happier during her nine months of marriage to a good but dull husband than she had ever been before. Her life was one of " short commons " : she was physically weak, her liver was always getting out of order, her " animal spirits " were invariably low. She saw her brother and sisters die in tragic succession : she was bereft of all family companionship and though she lived to be famous, her life, until she married, was pitiful. The picture of Mr. Brontë as a violent eccentric is now known to have been exaggerated and there is plenty of evidence of his quite ordinary behaviour and of the respect in which he was held in Haworth.

Nevertheless, we must still pity that solitary daughter who was conscientious to a point reached only by Victorian spinsters. Had the old man been really terrible, Charlotte might have left him ; she asserted herself when he overstepped the bounds in abuse of Mr. Nicholls as a future son-in-law. But Victorian parents rarely gave their children the opportunity of leaving them with a good conscience, and, in all ages, the trials of domestic life come from living, not with those who are obviously " impossible," for these can be deserted without compunction, but with those who are merely " trying " and whom, therefore, it is difficult to abandon.

Mr. Brontë and his son-in-law lived together, an odd couple linked by bereavement, for another six years after Charlotte's death. The old man died in 1861, in his eighty-fifth year. Mr. Nicholls then retired to Ireland and remarried. He died in 1906.

If Charlotte had lived longer, and if, as might have happened, circumstances had diverted her attention as a novelist from passionate love to other human relationships, she might have given the world as truthful an analysis of the conflict between filial feeling and a woman's longing for independence, or between wifely feeling and literary ambitions, as that she gave in *Jane Eyre* of the conflict between passion and duty. She took up her pen in childhood and in womanhood as an anodyne, and when the glamour of being Charlotte Bell Nicholls had worn off, she might, to some telling purpose, have taken it up again.

SOME BOOKS ON THE BRONTËS

Mrs. Gaskell : *Life and Works of Charlotte Brontë and Her Sisters*. Smith, Elder & Co.

Clement Shorter : *The Brontës : Life and Letters*. Hodder & Stoughton.

[*The Brontës : their Lives, Friendships and Correspondence*, edited by T. J. Wise and J. A. Symington (Blackwell, Oxford) incorporates Mr. Shorter's book.]

Madame Duclaux (A. Mary F. Robinson) : *Emily Brontë*.

Francis Leyland : *The Brontë Family, with special reference to Patrick Branwell Brontë*. Hurst & Blackett.

Augustine Birrell : *Charlotte Brontë*. Walter Scott Publishing Company.

Romer Wilson : *All Alone : the Life and Private History of Emily Jane Brontë*. Chatto & Windus.

Rosamund Langbridge : *Charlotte Brontë, a psychological study*.